Liv...g ..

Rolande A...
College Dublin, a...

counsellor since 1978. He was Assistant Director of the Alcohol/Chemical Dependence Programme at St Patrick's Hospital, where he worked for nearly 20 years. From 1997 to 1999 he was also Assistant Director of the Rutland Centre, a specialist residential addiction centre. He was one of the founding members and is a former public relations officer of the Irish Association of Alcohol and Addiction Counsellors. Since 1999, he has worked as a private counsellor in various settings including the Highfield Hospital Group, the Slievemore General Practice Clinic and FemPlus, all in Dublin. Since 2000 he has also been National Alcohol Project Director for the Irish College of General Practitioners. Rolande Anderson was a contributor to *Under the Weather: Coping with Alcohol Abuse and Alcoholism* by Dr John Cooney (Newleaf, 2002). He has lectured extensively on alcoholism and related topics, both at home and abroad. In addition to his many interests outside work, he prepares crosswords for various monthly publications in Ireland.

Overcoming Common Problems Series

Selected titles

A full list of titles is available from Sheldon Press,
36 Causton Street, London SW1P 4ST and on our website at
www.sheldonpress.co.uk

Asperger Syndrome in Adults
Dr Ruth Searle

The Assertiveness Handbook
Mary Hartley

Assertiveness: Step by step
Dr Windy Dryden and Daniel Constantinou

Backache: What you need to know
Dr David Delvin

Body Language: What you need to know
David Cohen

The Cancer Survivor's Handbook
Dr Terry Priestman

The Chronic Fatigue Healing Diet
Christine Craggs-Hinton

The Chronic Pain Diet Book
Neville Shone

Cider Vinegar
Margaret Hills

The Complete Carer's Guide
Bridget McCall

Confidence Works
Gladeana McMahon

Coping Successfully with Pain
Neville Shone

Coping Successfully with Period Problems
Mary-Claire Mason

Coping Successfully with Prostate Cancer
Dr Tom Smith

Coping Successfully with Psoriasis
Christine Craggs-Hinton

Coping Successfully with Ulcerative Colitis
Peter Cartwright

Coping Successfully with Varicose Veins
Christine Craggs-Hinton

Coping Successfully with Your Hiatus Hernia
Dr Tom Smith

Coping Successfully with Your Irritable Bowel
Rosemary Nicol

Coping When Your Child Has Cerebral Palsy
Jill Eckersley

Coping with Age-related Memory Loss
Dr Tom Smith

Coping with Birth Trauma and Postnatal Depression
Lucy Jolin

Coping with Bowel Cancer
Dr Tom Smith

Coping with Candida
Shirley Trickett

Coping with Chemotherapy
Dr Terry Priestman

Coping with Chronic Fatigue
Trudie Chalder

Coping with Coeliac Disease
Karen Brody

Coping with Compulsive Eating
Dr Ruth Searle

Coping with Diabetes in Childhood and Adolescence
Dr Philippa Kaye

Coping with Diverticulitis
Peter Cartwright

Coping with Eating Disorders and Body Image
Christine Craggs-Hinton

Coping with Epilepsy in Children and Young People
Susan Elliot-Wright

Coping with Family Stress
Dr Peter Cheevers

Coping with Gout
Christine Craggs-Hinton

Coping with Hay Fever
Christine Craggs-Hinton

Coping with Headaches and Migraine
Alison Frith

Coping with Hearing Loss
Christine Craggs-Hinton

Coping with Heartburn and Reflux
Dr Tom Smith

Coping with Kidney Disease
Dr Tom Smith

Coping with Life after Stroke
Dr Mareeni Raymond

Overcoming Common Problems Series

Overcoming Common Problems Series

Overcoming Common Problems

Living with a Problem Drinker
Your survival guide

ROLANDE ANDERSON

First published in Great Britain in 2010

Sheldon Press
36 Causton Street
London SW1P 4ST
www.sheldonpress.co.uk

British Library Cataloguing-in-Publication Data
A catalogue record for this book is available from the British Library

ISBN 978-1-84709-091-1

1 3 5 7 9 10 8 6 4 2

Typeset by Fakenham Photosetting Ltd, Fakenham, Norfolk
Printed in Great Britain by Ashford Colour Press

Produced on paper from sustainable forests

Contents

Acknowledgements

There are so many people to thank that it will not be possible to name them all. I can only hope that my friends and family will know how much they are all valued and how they have helped me with their love and support to do the job that I do and which I love. I also wish to thank my colleagues, past and present, who have been so helpful throughout my career.

There are some people that I simply have to mention:

The publishers, Sheldon Press, and Fiona Marshall, commissioning editor, in particular, for having faith in me and for giving me so much valuable advice and help in such a courteous way.

Dr J. G. Cooney, my first boss and mentor, for his ongoing friendship and guidance throughout my career.

Dr Denis Eustace, my great friend, whom I first met when starting off in St Patrick's Hospital, Dublin, and who has been such a devoted and loyal friend in so many ways ever since.

Dr Jane Marshall, consultant psychiatrist at the Maudsley Hospital, London, for helping me to understand treatment services in the UK.

Thanks to my friends from the Irish College of General Practitioners, especially Fionan O'Cuinneagáin, the CEO, Dr Michael Boland, GP, and also my good friend and colleague, Yvette Dalton, for helping with the diagrams and for proofing the book for me. They have all been greatly encouraging and supportive.

All the patients and family members that I have ever met who have taught me most of what I know about alcohol problems. I hope I have a lot more to meet and I know I have much more to learn.

Most especially I want to thank Barbara, my wife and my very best friend, for her devoted love, support and encouragement. Thanks also to our beloved children, Laura and Gareth, of whom we are so proud, and whom we love more than could ever be expressed.

Notes to the reader

While every reasonable care has been taken to check every word and sentence in this book, errors may still have occurred.

It is also probable that in time a great deal more will be known about this subject. In years to come, such knowledge may supersede some of these contents and hopefully improve on available help and helping methods.

No case example is exactly real in this book as changes have had to be made to ensure anonymity and confidentiality. The case illustrations are amalgams of reported events so that the issues depicted are very genuine. I believe they accurately reflect the type and intensity of complex dilemmas that confront family members in coping with alcohol problems and the struggles facing people where alcohol dominates relationships.

The family consequences of problem drinking, in general, and alcohol dependence, in particular, are the focus of this book. For the sake of convenience, the terms 'alcoholic' and 'alcoholism' and 'alcohol dependence' and 'addiction' are used interchangeably.

'He' and 'she' are used in alternate chapters for convenience, too, except where it is obvious that there are specific gender issues.

Chapter 1 is all about the wider context of alcohol problems for families. I have included an 'A to Z', Chapter 2, to ensure that some important aspects are highlighted in the book and as an easy, quick read of difficult issues. The titles of the rest of the chapters are self-explanatory, I trust.

At the end of most chapters I have included some frequently asked questions because they are indeed frequently asked by partners. I also wanted to ensure that other aspects are included or emphasized using this format.

The book does not include classic references but the sources of some articles and books, named in the text, are included in the References and further reading section at the end of the book.

Any readers who require further assistance are strongly recommended to seek out that help. They should consult the Useful addresses section.

It is never too late to seek help. It is a question of gathering up enough courage and trusting the process.

Introduction
Why write this book?

Having trained as a professional social worker in Trinity College Dublin, I have been working in this field as a specialist alcohol and addiction counsellor since 1978. In that time I have seen thousands upon thousands of people and their families in one-to-one sessions, marital interviews, family meetings and group therapy.

Most of my career has been spent in two of the leading treatment centres in Dublin. I ran a group for partners of in-patients every Tuesday for 18 years in St Patrick's Hospital. I worked there for nearly 20 years in total, and as the assistant director of the alcohol team for the last ten of those years. I was also the assistant director, for three years, in a specialist residential addiction centre, the Rutland Centre.

Since 1999, I have worked as a private counsellor in various settings including the Highfield Hospital Group, the Slievemore General Practice Clinic and FemPlus, in different parts of Dublin. In addition I have been the National Alcohol Project Director for the Irish College of General Practitioners from 2000 to date. I have lectured extensively on this and other related topics, at home and abroad.

In all this time I have gained so much experience, gleaned so much knowledge and learned so many lessons from the people I have seen. I have also been blessed to have had wonderful colleagues and friends who have taught me so much. I have constantly been enthralled and mystified by the difficult situations that people have to contend with, their courage in opening up and dealing with them and the incredible personal resources that allow people to survive – and in many cases to thrive – despite the hand that they were dealt in adult life. In many cases they have also had to contend with extraordinarily difficult personal histories in their formative years.

As a result of such rich exposure to family issues I felt compelled to try to capture and record some of the simple and complex nuances in families where alcohol problems occur. I am very conscious that access to professional help is often difficult and sometimes very expensive in certain areas. Perhaps some people may gain help and strength from reading this book, which is an attempt to illustrate my knowledge about families and alcohol problems.

Some years ago I wrote a chapter on the family for *Under the Weather*, a book which became a bestseller in Ireland. My chapter was a descriptive account of alcohol problems and their impact on family life. In *Living with a Problem Drinker*, I explore these matters in much more detail.

However, in this written effort I wanted to go a little further and explore other, more complicated areas. I needed to write about the impact of family life and unhappy relationships on the development and continuance of alcohol problems. This is not easy as there are so many complex variables and multiple factors in the unfolding stories of addiction. Where possible, these situations are illustrated by case examples that have been carefully doctored to avoid any possible exposure of real people. I am also very conscious of the possible hurt such analysis might cause to certain people. However, these matters must be written about and explored, in my view. My only intention is to illuminate such issues in order to help people to heal.

I believe the general public is confused by some of the terms that are used in this area, such as 'co-dependence', 'enabling' and 'denial'. I also wanted to explain a few of these, as best I could, in my own way.

This is my first book, and as such it represents the removal of a large 'monkey from my back'. I have been encouraged to write by patients, friends, colleagues and family for many years – years of telling people to 'go for it' and not taking my own advice! It has been my ambition to write about alcohol and family life since I started on my career path. I have been privileged in my life to work in this area and to meet so many people who have trusted me with their innermost secrets, thoughts and feelings: that is, their own personal 'crown jewels'. These remain safe with me, of course, and I now publicly thank them for their faith, courage and openness.

There are wider issues too that have prompted me to write. Alcohol problems are pervasive in our society. Their tendrils are so damaging to health and family life, and as such are the most prevalent public health issue in the United Kingdom and Ireland. Millions of people and their families are locked in the throes of coping with alcohol problems, with devastating consequences for their personal health, well-being and safety. Marital and relationship breakdown is a direct and regular result of alcohol problems, as are a host of minor and serious illnesses, child abuse and neglect, domestic violence, sexual problems and abuse, as well as major mental health problems including depression and suicide. One would think that with such wide-scale destruction, comprehensive and elaborate treatment and counselling services would be available, as well as coherent strategies to reduce the pain. The truth, however, is that an alarming 'blind eye' is turned to alcohol problems and their tragic consequences, and mere token attempts are offered by the powers that be to deal effectively with the problem. Public treatment and counselling services are at best deemed hit-and-miss in many regional areas. At worst, they are totally absent.

If mental health is the Cinderella of public health services in terms of funding, then alcohol treatment facilities are one of the ugly sisters! Denial is entrenched and ingrained at every level: individual, family and societal. The drinks industry, with its vested interests and bottom-line profit requirements, continues to have too much power and influence over government policy. Governments seem afraid to upset or discommode it in any way. The industry's pithy media messages, such as 'Enjoy alcohol responsibly', may appear to resemble public health information but are in fact little more than advertising, and utterly cynical in my view. I believe the industry should not be allowed to use them. Meanwhile, in reality, people with alcohol problems and their family members struggle badly and in some cases die, relationships break up and sadly many children are damaged for life because they are not properly protected and do not get appropriate help.

This book is written for people stuck in alcohol-fuelled unhappy relationships. I sincerely hope it will be a catalyst for change, and will move some people away from the suffocating spiral of addictive patterns and behaviours. My motives are purely and simply to provide information and direct help to those who are suffering. I want to encourage people to seek appropriate help and to be able to regain some control or maybe even more control over their own lives and aspirations.

1

Context

The title of this book was originally going to be *Family Matters*. It was to be a play on words. Family matters, most people agree, and family matters that involve secrets or deep guilt and shame are often very difficult to sort out, or indeed to understand.

On deeper reflection, however, it was agreed that the book should be a guide for people trapped in unhappy relationships where alcohol plays a major role in the problems, hence the final title. For many people it is indeed only a matter of survival. Alcohol can absolutely shatter families. For others, however, there is considerable hope, as people do recover from alcohol problems and so too do their partners. Sometimes they recover together, sometimes separately. The emphasis within this book is on partners, though you will have seen that there is a chapter written to highlight the impact on children.

From the outset it should be noted that the majority of people in society derive support, love, strong bonds and intimate, consistent relationships from their families. Within every family unit, events and incidents go on behind closed doors that can be positive and negative for all concerned. Some of these negative events and incidents are well hidden, secret and traumatic. Family matters are deep and complex.

So too are alcohol problems. They occur in every street and locality in society. Alcohol-related problems impact hugely and adversely on everyone caught up in the close-knit arena that makes up family life. When a family member drinks to excess or drinks in a dependent manner, the repercussions for the health, safety and well-being of all concerned are usually profound and long-lasting. Having a problem drinker in the family means emotional suffering.

The term 'problem drinker' was selected as it covers the wide gamut of people who encounter problems with alcohol, not just those who are addicted to alcohol.

What is a 'problem drinker'?

It has always been accepted that alcoholism is a major factor in family distress and illness. Nowadays there is a clearer understanding and awareness that it is not just alcoholism that causes the damage: a whole range of alcohol problems can create difficulties for family members too. So binge drinking, one-off episodes of excess drinking and of course alcohol dependence can all be implicated in family upheaval and breakdown. Hazardous, harmful and dependent drinking are all sources of mayhem within relationships.

However, there is another important side to this story which is difficult to describe. Can family relationships cause or contribute to alcohol problems? How do family life and family dynamics, in certain cases, add to the creation of alcohol problems? Such issues are discussed and described later on. These are tricky and sensitive questions but they have to be aired and debated if we want to reach a full understanding of the situation for the partner. The hope is that the contents of this book will help some people to reduce or stop their drinking, while helping others to get professional and other help to cope with a loved one. It is also the intention to help people gain insight into the enmeshed family systems that are toxic to the emotional health of all parts of that system.

Which comes first, the chicken or the egg? This classic conundrum was never as relevant as in the case of families coping with alcohol problems. Do alcohol problems precede family problems? Do alcohol problems result from family problems? The truth is probably yes to both presuppositions, though every case is very different.

One aspect is crystal clear, and that is that alcohol is the cause of a great number of societal ills. As such, the harm permeates through all layers of community life, including the home.

What of the impact on children? This is surely the 'emperor's new clothes' within our society. Two blind eyes are turned to the damage caused to children by alcohol problems at most levels within our society. The silent and loud cries of anguish of children who are caught up in families where alcohol predominates are largely unheard and ignored. The devastation inflicted on children at all stages of their development, resulting from alcohol and disturbed family systems, is profound and has far-reaching implications. Such suffering can sculpt their own patterns of behaviour as adults and, sadly, the cycle of further alcohol problems within the family often continues if the underlying issues are not resolved early enough.

Is alcoholism a disease?

Before describing the impact of alcohol on the family and the impact of the family on alcohol problems, it is important to discuss alcohol risk categories so that the full context is properly established. One would need the wisdom of Solomon to be able to explain the complex arguments and nuances that appear on both sides of the disease debate divide. Is it a bad habit? Is it a form of dependence? Is it a lack of something within the person? Is it a personality disorder? Is it a manifestation of a deeper issue or issues? Is it a 'hole in the soul' or a lack of spirituality? Is it caused by the drinks industry? Is it simply the case that a certain percentage of people who consume alcohol will become dependent? If alcoholism is a disease, is it hereditary? Is it simply another addiction? If alcoholism is a disease, why do we not also call other types of substance abuse a disease? Should heroin addiction be called 'heroinism', for example?

All these questions and many more besides are the stuff of theses, doctorates and hot-headed disputes. They are important issues, though, for the individual problem drinker and family members too. Suffice to say, at this stage, that there are three outstanding issues that need to be acknowledged:

- First, whatever it is described as, I have never yet met a person who wanted to become dependent on alcohol.
- Second, even if alcoholism is accepted as a disease, the disease concept should not be used to prevent a person from dealing with the consequences of or accepting responsibility for the problems that ensue.
- Third, and perhaps most important in the context of this book, problem drinkers and families need help and support no matter what the condition is called or how it is categorized.

People with alcohol problems and family members on the front line of these arguments and conflicts are also equally divided about the merits and demerits of the disease debate. Numerous partners and children have related how their loved ones have denied responsibility for serious aspects of their behaviour because of their understanding of the disease concept. They cannot be held responsible for events while under the influence of alcohol because they are suffering from a disease – this is the type of argument used to avoid personal responsibility.

The victims of alcohol-fuelled hatred, anger, abuse, fear, neglect and threats do not care that much whether the problem is labelled as alcoholism or not. Their only focus, while in the war zone, is survival. If a family member is the victim of a head-butt by a relative who is drunk, it really does not matter to the wounded person at that time whether or not the perpetrator is sick, bad or crazy, as the hurt and damage caused is still the same no matter what the diagnosis. And, of course, in addition to physical abuse, families suffer severe and regular verbal and emotional violence as well.

The following are typical comments of supporters of this view of alcoholism as an illness: 'I am not responsible for screaming at you because I have an illness'; 'The booze made me hit you'; 'If you had not talked to me while I was drunk it would not have happened.' Many family members simply accept that alcoholism is a disease, in blind faith, or once again state that they do not care what it is called as long as their loved one, or once-loved one, recovers.

So the disease debate rages on and continues to be a very vexed issue and a subject that causes grief within homes and in academia, as well as among specialists in this field. It remains an important question to answer, however, for many reasons, not least because the approach to people with 'alcoholism' is often determined by diagnostic terms. Insurance cover for treatment, for example, as well as location of treatment or no treatment at all, is often decided as a result of such mind-sets.

Funding resources to combat drinking consequences, as well as the attitude of all healthcare professionals in this area, are ulti- mately determined by this debate. Historically, people dependent on alcohol were treated as outcasts and as morally reprehensible and undesirable. They were the 'personality lepers' within our society. This attitude tended to make the problem even more secretive. The advent of the 'disease' concept meant that treatment was more widely available and that problem drinkers were much more likely to avail themselves of such treatment. Critics say that in this way a social problem was medicalized and a new industry of private treat- ment was developed. Evidence for this view exists in the sense that there has been very poor provision of treatment services for public patients, whereas, if an individual has the means or the insurance to benefit from private healthcare facilities, there is a proliferation of such options.

Many hold to the view of alcoholism as a bio-psycho-social disease. This represents a modern approach to any disease or sickness, holding that biological, psychological and social factors all combine to con- tribute to the development of alcoholism and may all contribute to a successful resolution or to a failure to resolve the problem. This view mostly reflects my own thinking on the disease debate.

People with alcohol problems are not immune to other medical, social and mental health problems and are in fact more likely to suffer additional consequences unless the alcohol problem is successfully addressed.

Risk categories

Years ago it was relatively simple – one was either alcoholic or not. Today, we try to be more sophisticated and talk of a continuum of risk and a range of alcohol problems. Thus there are four main risk categories: low-risk drinking, hazardous drinking, harmful drinking and dependence. They are depicted in Figure 1.

This is an attempt to categorize people in every population in terms of risk criteria for alcohol problems. I think it is a very useful tool to help people decide where they might stand.

The definitions of these categories are as follows.

Low-risk drinking

Consumption of small amounts of alcohol that is unlikely to cause any form of harm should present drinking patterns persist. This risk category includes people who do not drink alcohol at all and those who used to drink but now abstain or drink very small amounts.

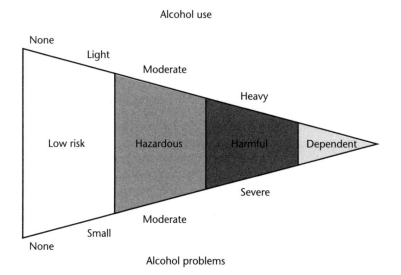

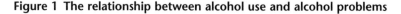

Figure 1 The relationship between alcohol use and alcohol problems

Hazardous drinking

A level of consumption or pattern of drinking that is likely to result in harm should present drinking habits persist. This includes any drinking by pregnant women, children under 16 years of age, and people who are ill or receiving treatment or who are performing activities that are not advised when drinking. Hazardous drinking can include binge drinking.

Harmful drinking

A pattern of drinking that causes damage to health, either physical or mental. Includes heavy episodic or binge drinking.

Dependence

A cluster of psychological, behavioural and cognitive phenomena in which the use of alcohol takes on a much higher priority for a given individual than other behaviours that once had greater value. Definitions of dependence vary slightly across the world. According to the *Diagnostic and Statistical Manual of Mental Disorders* in the United States (DSM IV) a patient has to satisfy three of the following signs of dependence over a 12-month period:

- tolerance to alcohol;
- withdrawal symptoms on stopping drinking;
- loss of control (use of alcohol in larger amounts for longer periods than intended);
- persistent desire and unsuccessful attempts to cut down use;
- spending time obtaining alcohol or in recovery from alcohol use;
- giving up or reducing social, occupational and recreational pursuits because of alcohol;
- continuing use despite knowledge of alcohol-related harm.

Although Figure 1 is not exactly scientific and clinical judgement is still very important in making assessments for such risk categories, this model of understanding represents a vast improvement on what we had before. From a public health perspective most concern is within the hazardous and harmful categories, as these involve the largest percentage of any population.

The key practical aspect of this risk continuum, as depicted in Figure 1, is how people in each category should be advised to behave with regard to alcohol. People in the hazardous category are usually advised to cut down on their drinking. There is more controversy when it comes to advice offered to those in the harmful category.

They should certainly reduce their consumption but, depending on the degree of harm, may well be advised to cut out alcohol altogether. People with a diagnosis of dependence are routinely advised to abstain totally. Such advice is dispensed by counsellors, GPs, psychiatrists or other healthcare professionals using a combination of examination, questionnaires and clinical experience to determine the person's risk category.

Can people in the harmful and dependence categories control their drinking? This is yet another huge area of controversy. The abstinence versus controlled drinking debate is alive and well. Obviously people will make up their own minds because of or in spite of 'experts', but it is clearly a very important decision for anyone who has experienced serious problems as a result of alcohol consumption.

Consider these two case scenarios:

A man in his forties, who presents with only a few of the signs and symptoms of dependence, confides that when he drinks on occasions he physically assaults his partner. This has happened four or five times with severe consequences obviously for her but also for him. He also relates that he does not ever remember the incidents owing to alcohol memory blackouts.

Another lady in her fifties has serious liver damage. She has been diagnosed with liver cirrhosis. Again, she has only a few of the symptoms of dependence.

Most practitioners would advise both to abstain from alcohol, I believe.

Other situations are not so clear, and advice on reduction or stopping completely has to be tailored to each person who comes looking for help.

There are all sorts of other aspects to consider when assessing someone's alcohol risk status. Are there mental health issues? Alcohol and depression are close cousins, as are anxiety and alcohol; they are both cause and effect of alcohol problems. Is there a hereditary aspect? Many people have parents or grandparents with alcohol-related problems. Has the person tried to stop before or had previous attempts at treatment? How much do other incidents, including family background, influence the way in which a person drinks? People often have complicated histories involving prolonged and severe abuse of many kinds. Is there a connection to such histories and alcohol problems?

How many people are in each category? We do not have accurate figures so it is difficult to guess. Judging from many reports and research conducted by the Irish College of General Practitioners, we could speculate that in the UK and Ireland:

- 30 to 40 per cent of drinkers are in the low-risk category;
- 20 to 40 per cent are drinking hazardously;
- 10 to 20 per cent may be drinking harmfully;
- 6 to 10 per cent of drinkers are dependent.

It is clear, therefore, that a large number of partners and children are seriously affected. The Alcohol Harm Reduction Strategy for England indicated in 2004 that 1.3 million children in England were significantly affected.

Family members can be scarred by the drinking behaviour of people in the hazardous, harmful and dependent categories. Even one-off drunken incidents can be very damaging to the health and well-being of family members. For example, a man has sex with someone on a night out when drunk and then contracts a sexually transmitted disease; he will literally bring home health problems for his partner, and of course may damage trust for ever if she discovers his infidelity.

The people of the UK and Ireland have a long association with heavy drinking. Speaking about the Irish, though he could just as easily have said Welsh, English or Scottish, the well-known temperance reformer the Very Reverend Theobald Mathew in 1840 encapsulated our relationship with alcohol as follows:

> In truth not only were our countrymen remarkable for their intemperate use of intoxicating liquors but intemperance had already entered into and formed a part of the national character. An Irishman and a drunkard had become synonymous terms. Whenever he was to be introduced in character he would be represented habited in rags, bleeding at the nose and waving a shillelagh.

Apart from the shillelagh, this could almost have been written about people who are drunk on our streets on any given night of the week these days. How far have we come since 1840?

Frequently asked questions

What is the difference between harm caused by alcohol problems within families and other forms of harm in families brought on by mental health problems or drug abuse or physical illness, or by violence or other forms of abuse?

In many cases there is not that much difference, and in fact the resulting harms are often very similar. Alcohol problems are hard to detect in families as families go to elaborate lengths to conceal the situation and to keep it secret because of guilt and shame. Like other forms of substance abuse, this problem is considered by many to be self-inflicted, and as such it is perhaps more shameful than, for example, mental health problems. One of the key factors in understanding alcohol abuse and the harm done by alcohol in families is that, in many ways and in different respects, alcohol abuse is socially sanctioned. There is incredible tolerance in society for abusive drinking behaviour. People are excused on the basis that they did not really mean what they said or did because they were drinking or drunk. It is as if there is a collective denial of the harm caused by alcohol. The fact that alcohol, unlike cocaine for example, is a legal drug means that its negative consequences are minimized.

I have heard people being described as functional alcoholics and wonder what that means. My partner is alcoholic in my opinion and is certainly not functioning.

I do not like this term 'functioning alcoholic' at all. It is contradictory and misleading. I do not believe it is accurate, and it implies that someone who, by definition, is behaving out of control is in fact coping fine. I think the term has been introduced to describe people who are *apparently* functioning, without any real detailed examination or analysis of their personal lives. It is well known that people with alcohol problems will try to give the impression that all is well to throw people off the scent. They turn up for work on time, for example. However, if partners or children are consulted, a whole different perspective might be offered. People with alcohol problems are not out of control all the time and have periods of control and relative normality, and these periods serve to confuse the situation for partners and healthcare professionals. One of the biggest problems in detecting alcohol problems at primary care level is that the stereotype of the problem drinker is rarely appropriate. If someone's drinking is harmful or dependent, they are not functioning in any real sense of that word and things are likely to deteriorate over time.

2

An A to Z of issues for the partner

I decided to write an A to Z of issues for the partner of the problem drinker as a way of allowing readers to dip in and out of this book and to get a flavour of what is to come in the following chapters. Of course, I could have picked many other words for each letter but most of the following issues are elaborated upon in later chapters.

A for angst

Angst could be defined as a combination of anxiety and stress, and living with alcohol problems involves a great deal of it: regular, ongoing and intense. Some writers have talked of alcoholics suffering from 'Deep Nameless Anxiety' or DNA. This is a type of unpleasant foreboding that is almost always present. You cannot quite put your finger on it or describe specifically what it is or where it is coming from. The partner suffers the same type of angst, I believe. He does not know when the next incident is going to occur so he is in a constant state of alert. The angst is also due to worry, fear and exhaustion.

B for broken

Broken dreams, broken hopes, broken bones, broken sleep, broken trust, broken promises, broken hearts! What a horrible whirlpool of loss and hurt in a relationship that once, maybe, was functioning well. Partners have an array of different types of brokenness and ultimately, if things are not resolved, they too feel utterly smashed as persons within themselves. They develop a keen sense of failure. Brokenness starts off with brittleness, and constant wear and tear on the emotional bones without any help or resolution leads to a type of 'emotional osteoporosis' (osteoporosis is a medical condition where bones are easily broken; ironically, using such a metaphor in this context, it can be brought on by alcohol).

C for criticism

In keeping with the previous theme, it is often said that 'sticks and stones can break my bones but names can never hurt me'. Another interpretation of that old saying is 'sticks and stones can break my bones but names can wound for ever'. Perhaps both statements are true in different situations and for different personalities. The partner is often subject to a constant flow of vitriolic criticism and name-calling. Perhaps the alcoholic unloads her own inadequacies on her partner when drunk, but it is very hard to live with. The unfortunate reality is that the partner may come to believe that the abuse is accurate or even part-accurate. 'You are useless, you are cold and unfeeling, you are stupid, you are a piece of rubbish, you and your family are interfering losers, you will never make anything of yourself, you are ugly, you are only good for one thing, and you are a waste of space.'

D for depression

Depression is common among partners, but we need to be very careful again here with definitions. Almost always the partner suffers from very low feelings and exasperation. Constant angst and criticism, as already described, together with tiredness and exhaustion, ruin self-confidence and self-esteem. This can all lead to forms of clinical depression. Sometimes the cause of such reactive depression is not examined, understood or explored by healthcare professionals, who may only treat the presenting symptoms so that the partner may find himself on antidepressant medication. It is debatable whether or not, in these circumstances, this form of treatment on its own is helpful, and even whether it is necessary. Partners are at risk of self-harm, attempted suicide and suicide at certain times and in certain situations. Therefore, they definitely require help, and sometimes this should include medication alongside other forms of assistance.

E for excuses

After an incident has occurred, the partner, looking for some type of explanation for the behaviour, is often confronted by all sorts of rationalizations. The excuses for the drinking and the ensuing consequences can be flimsy – 'Someone asked me to go for a drink' – or a bit more complex – 'It is all your fault. If you had been at home, as you said you would be, I would not have gone drinking.' The partner may believe the excuses and blame himself, or dismiss them and get into a deeper row. This represents a classic 'no-win' situation. The partner also becomes expert at making excuses for events and incidents. 'We can't go to the party because my partner has a high temperature,' says he, for fear that she will drink and destroy the evening.

F for fear

The most predominant emotion in living with alcohol problems is fear. Partners are in a perpetual state of fear. Many alcoholics struggle to understand this, because in some cases they rightly claim that they are gentle and harmless when drunk. But fear is much more than the worry about being physically hurt. It involves fear of being left alone, of the impact of all of this on the family, of criticism from outsiders, of being judged, of not having enough money, of injury to the alcoholic, of the future, and of where it will all end. Partners are also deeply fearful of when the next episode will happen and try to predict the sequence of events. For example, if a wedding or other big social event is arranged, a lot of emotional effort will be put into preparing for the possibility that the partner will drink. Alas, alcoholics are, by definition, unpredictable when in active addiction and rarely announce the date of their next binge or bout. Even if they did, the fear would still be present.

G for guilt

Yet another common emotion is a sense of guilt for the occurrence of another incident or for the whole situation. Why should the partner feel guilty? What could he possibly have done to cause it? I suppose if you are in a relationship there is a type of shared guilt when things go wrong. This could be described as guilt by association. If your partner assaults someone when drunk it is not easy to stand back and simply say it was her responsibility and not take on any responsibility or shame. There is a deeper form of guilt, though, and that is to do with inaction. 'I should have done something to prevent it.' Such guilt is often compounded by a feeling of guilt from other events in the partner's life. Sometimes, too, the partner has been trained in guilt by being raised in a home where drinking problems were prevalent. Would you ring the police if you knew your partner was going out to drink and drive? Many partners do, but it constitutes a major moral and emotional struggle to come to this decision.

H for hopelessness

Martin Seligman, the American psychologist and author, coined a wonderful term for institutionalization: 'learned helplessness'. This is where individuals become powerless in an institution, such as a hospital, when they are there for a lengthy period of time, because everything is done for them and they lose their ability to do things for themselves. Well, marriage is an institution, and when relationships go wrong this state of emotional paralysis can result. I think the partner of a problem drinker can suffer from 'learned hopelessness' as well, however, and by this I mean that he has lost hope over many long years and does not believe that anything can or will change. He just survives. This sense of utter powerlessness is obviously very damaging to the person's health and welfare. In certain cases it is a recipe for active self-harm.

I for illness

There is no doubt that partners suffer from a range of health problems. Emotional indigestion is common. The partner simply cannot stomach (sorry!) his daily diet and develops all sorts of related symptoms as a result. So, ulcers, headaches, skin problems, diarrhoea, constipation, back pain and many more common complaints, and perhaps some other more serious illnesses too, might be partly caused or exacerbated by alcoholism in the family. Two other aspects are relevant here. Sadly, the partner may be so beaten down emotionally that when he gets ill he does not feel able to take time out. He may put off going to his doctor, with the result that often his symptoms will deteriorate. In addition, typically he gets little sympathy, tolerance or support from the alcoholic in active addiction.

J for jealousy

Jealousy is often a feature in relationships that are dominated by alcohol problems. There are, as usual, both simple and complex explanations for such emotions. The simplest is that the person who is drinking too much has some insight and sees herself as unattractive, unstable and undesirable. If she sees her partner talking to someone else, her imagination and deep self-loathing are likely to run riot. Jealousy and awful rows can follow. Many disputes in pubs often start in this way. It is not uncommon to hear of someone being struck or verbally assaulted for innocently talking to a partner. Jealousy can also be a sign of a deeper problem that emanates from insecurity or a type of mental health problem. In rare cases paranoid jealousy can occur and this involves danger to the partner. The partner himself is often jealous of what he sees as 'normal couples'.

K for killjoy

Pleasant, supposed-to-be-happy occasions are often ruined by alcohol. After a lovely day together, for example, one word can lead to another and a full-blown argument can suddenly erupt. This can happen in every relationship, of course, but is more likely to occur when one of the couple is a problem drinker. The conflict is probably rooted in some form of drunken logic, and is therefore unlikely to be resolved by talking. Holidays with an active alcoholic are particularly fraught for the partner. Tales of coming home early from abroad, or of being left alone in a hotel room without knowing where she might be, or of hours spent in some Accident and Emergency department, or of drunken encounters with the local police, are commonplace.

L for loneliness

I could have easily chosen 'love' for this category but decided to focus on loneliness. In Alcoholics Anonymous circles there is a catchphrase: 'HALT'. These letters stand for hungry, angry, lonely and tired. The idea is that these are possible triggers for a relapse, and the alcoholic has to deal with these emotions and situations carefully. The partner suffers greatly from loneliness too. He is often on his own at home or in party situations because his partner is 'out of it' or emotionally unavailable through drinking and hangovers. He is unlikely, without help, to seek support from friends or family and therefore has an increased sense of isolation. In other cases partners report that they have made their own independent lives but still harbour a deep sense of loneliness as they are obliged to handle issues and events without any real support. Without help, isolation gets worse over time.

M for manipulations

Everyone in the drama surrounding alcohol problems becomes expert at manipulative behaviour. Perhaps that is a slight exaggeration, but manipulative behaviour is very common by partner and problem drinker alike. In the partner's case, the manipulations are often practical and to do with avoidance of angry disputes or to manage short-term peace. He might promise things to get her to change or bribe her in some way or other. He will entice his wife with sex, for example, to get her to go to bed when drunk so that she will sleep if off and not wake the children. In the case of the alcoholic, typically she will create some sort of argument to justify her drinking in her own mind and later can blame him for starting it.

N for nightmares

Night is always the worst time for worrying. Tiredness, combined with reflecting on the events of the day and the fear of what tomorrow might bring, often leads to sleep disturbance for partners. They are perhaps lying beside someone who seems like a total stranger, in a drunken stupor and maybe snoring noisily. They are unable to sleep properly because they are so angry, deeply hurt and full of resentment. Many are prescribed sleeping tablets, without any proper exploration of the reason for the insomnia. Sometimes the doctor asks about underlying causes but is met with denial and plausible excuses. Actual nightmares are regular for the partner, though the real-life nightmare of living with active alcoholism is more pertinent to sleep problems and everything else in this A to Z.

O for obsessions

Obsessing about the person with the problem and related incidents and accidents is frequently cited by partners in therapy as another desperately unpleasant consequence of living with alcoholism. He can think of almost nothing else and fails to concentrate on other things like work or the children. This is of course entirely understandable. The focus narrows from other aspects of life to the aim of trying to stop her drinking and of limiting the damage when it does happen. The danger with such obsessions is that the partner utterly neglects himself and others around him and becomes a full-time carer, trying vainly to control the situation. He is in danger of becoming a 'control freak'. He behaves like a police officer trying to detect the next 'crime' or a surveillance expert trying to catch her out. The effort involved in managing these obsessions is huge and leads to further problems, as the obsessive behaviour tends to take over every area of his life.

P for practical problems

In trying to throw light on the psychological and emotional consequences of alcohol problems, it is all too easy to neglect or ignore
practical realities. The ordinary day-to-day issues that have to be negotiated are still present despite the problem drinking. Things that many
of us take for granted become problematic when alcohol problems are
part of the scene. These are far-ranging and involve: financial worries
(paying bills, budgeting, having money for special events, debt, talking
to the bank or credit union, dealing with loan agencies and sometime
loan sharks), getting from A to B (she is off the road because of drunk
driving or there are no funds for transport), baby-sitting problems (she
does not come home on time so he can't go out, or has to warn baby-
sitters that she might be drunk if she does come home), dinners burned
or uneaten, inadequate accommodation (so he cannot move out of the
bedroom when things are bad), and all sorts of other basic issues.

Q for quick fix

Just as addiction is all about short-term relief and long-term pain, so
too the partner tends to go for the quick-fix option. There may be
few long-term goals or none. The only aim is to get over the acute
problem. Other writers have described this phenomenon as being like
having an elephant in your sitting room. You clean up after it and you
feed it, but you humour it and try hard to prevent it from moving. If
it does shift position, you sort out the structural and practical damage
that ensues and try to get it back to where it was with the minimum
disruption to the family. How the elephant got there, or the fact that
it needs to be removed from the home altogether or reduced in size or
impact, is rarely recognized or addressed. You put a sticking plaster on
the problem and hope it will go away of its own accord. You only react
to situations and events; you are not able to plan properly.

R for rights

When romance has died in a relationship and there are few or no needs
being met, the partner can feel completely lost and, as noted, without
hope. He may believe he has no rights, or has not had time or space to
consider his own rights. To break free from this impasse he may need
to get all sorts of outside independent advice and help. He might need
advice from money specialists. He should probably also be encouraged
to receive legal advice. This is obviously a big step for someone who

has been down-trodden, and many partners are fearful that by talking to a family law solicitor they are starting procedures that they cannot stop. They have often also been warned not to get such advice or 'I will leave you penniless' or 'I will reveal the truth about you in public.' They need help to resist such threats. In fact they often discover when consulting with outside legal advocates that they do have some legal options. Such awareness can be very empowering and help the person to get moving.

S for sexual problems

A whole book could be written on this topic! Suffice to say here that sexual problems are multiple in most cases of alcohol problems. The partner is expected to perform even though he may feel ill at the very idea of sleeping with his partner when she is drunk. Sometimes he may go for the quick fix again here and 'undergo' sexual contact or intercourse to attempt to keep things on an even keel and not cause further disagreements. He can therefore be sleeping with someone who smells of stale alcohol, has poor general hygiene and shows little or no sensitivity. In this state the sexual act is at best clumsy and at worst traumatic. Sometimes this leads to more anger and frustration. Infidelity is common enough on both sides, and unfair accusations of affairs are often hurled in both directions. Rape within the relationship is a sad reality for some partners and under-reported to the police.

T for trust

In many cases, people in relationships are only conscious of the presence or absence of trust when it has been broken. Perhaps we all put too much weight or importance on trust in relationships, but partners can be destroyed by the inability to trust. Listening to lies and broken promises is part of the deterioration in trust. Failure to do what was asked or expected adds to it, while outrageous behaviour is the tin lid on the demolition of trust. Strange phone calls or mysterious emails or texts from a stranger who seems to know your partner well may or may not be innocent, but lead to an erosion of trust. The partner too can be untrustworthy, planning and plotting behind the other person's back or seeking solace from someone who shows care and attentiveness. Trust takes much work and a long time to re-establish, even if the problem drinking is solved.

U for unacceptable

If the partner starts to accept unacceptable behaviour, apparently getting over it in the short term, this can often lead to a spiral of further episodes of unacceptable behaviour. The informal rules of the original relationship are now fundamentally changed. The goal-posts have been moved. As far as the perpetrator is concerned there is some form of tacit consent and acceptance of the unacceptable behaviour. The partner's choice is to put up and shut up, on the one hand, or go over old ground, renegotiate and risk World War III, on the other. Some of the unacceptable behaviours are relatively minor in his eyes. Other things that he has endured are so shameful and embarrassing that he feels he cannot possibly discuss them with another living soul. They can burn away deep inside him, but remain secret. Sometimes things happen so fast that he does not have time to realize that he would normally consider the behaviour unacceptable. Such issues can fester away inside and keep him stuck in a destructive relationship.

V for violence

Men and women can be battered physically in alcoholic relationships. Some of the beatings are horrific; all are humiliating and demoralizing. Most of such violence is hidden and covered up, although the physical impact of some outbursts of violence is so obvious that it is impossible to disguise the marks. Not all alcoholics are physically violent, though in my view all are abusive in some sense when actively drinking. Emotional abuse, name-calling, put-downs, shouting, intimidation, staring, sulking and angry silences are all used and could certainly be described as violent actions. The partner can be equally culpable in this regard, and I have heard of many accounts of violence inflicted on the drinker when she is drunk or 'out of it'. In many cases she is not aware of the source of her physical hurt when she sobers up because she has forgotten what happened, and he is left with feelings of guilt and remorse.

W for wishing

Worry and angst clearly feature in the lives of people living with problem drinking, who also spend a lot of wasted time wishing and hoping that things might somehow change. They fantasize that they will win the Lottery or that they will get over the next stage in life and then they will make changes. 'When my children are grown up, I will leave her then', or 'I will move to another area', or 'I will keep her away from people who have a bad influence on her'. The unfortunate reality is that if, for whatever possible noble reason, you wait that long for things to change, the patterns are usually so well established that change is less likely to occur. We know that we all tend to be creatures of habit, but we need to stand back and reflect and then take action if things are actually to change. Wishing alone is most unlikely to alter your situation.

Nothing changes if nothing changes.

X for X-rated events and incidents

Within the life span of a couple coping with alcoholism, all sorts of incidents occur that are very personal and extreme. Most examples are so specific that disclosure would threaten people's confidentiality, but in broad terms I am mostly thinking of bizarre violence or sexual behaviour. In one case a man was locked in a freezing shed for several hours because he was deemed to be 'so cold' by his drunken partner in her drunken logic. In another case a woman was humiliatingly 'examined' for evidence of infidelity whenever she would come home after being out for a night. Threats of suicide involving brinkmanship are also included in this category. Reckless honesty fits into this section too. For example, while she was in treatment for alcoholism a man told his partner about his multiple affairs in the past. Perhaps this was to ease his own guilt. Later, perhaps understandably, their relationship ended.

Y for yesterday

Couples need help to get through the obstacle course that is recovery, and it is a major effort to learn to forgive. Sometimes it is impossible, however, and certainly equally hard to forget. Yet despite all of the previous traumatic issues and events, many couples make full recoveries and learn to accommodate the traumatic past. Some people choose to move on or manage difficult issues by not naming them or by confining them to history. This is a tribute to the enduring nature of people and their ability to cope in the face of extreme problems. Dealing with issues as events of the past and letting go of hurts and insults is essential if the couple have any chance of recovery together. Therapy can help greatly but must be very sensitively handled if serious pitfalls are to be avoided.

Z for zero

Well, what else could I use for the letter Z? A loved one going from 'hero to zero' is the sad experience of many partners. From being courted and loved, in most cases, and having all sorts of aspirations and expectations, to a life of worry and anxiety and ultimate bereavement and loss due to alcohol problems in the relationship is a very unfortunate journey. The only mistake some partners make in this situation is to be capable of love. The emptiness of broken dreams can make some feel so empty that they feel like nothing.

Help is available, and despite all of the above, people can recover, with or without their partner.

3

Does my partner have a problem with alcohol? Is he or she an alcoholic?

> There was a little girl who had a little curl
> Right in the middle of her forehead,
> And when she was good she was very very good
> And when she was bad she was horrid.

Living with someone who has an alcohol problem, in most cases, is much like the sentiments contained in this well-known old nursery rhyme. People with alcohol problems are the nicest, warmest, most sensitive people when sober, the moodiest, most argumentative and cranky people, typically, when drunk.

One of the greatest urban myths is *in vino veritas* – the truth comes out in wine (and drink in general!). It is so hurtful to family members, friends, work colleagues and acquaintances, and nothing could be further from the truth. When someone is drunk he or she actually sees a distorted picture, like the blurred image you see if you look through the thick glass of a bottle. If your partner is drunk, in his drunken distorted logic he will tell you some 'home truth', as he sees it, when he is out of control. Probably this is because he feels so bad about himself that he wants to put you on the back foot, or maybe it is because the normal default human sensitivity button is not working properly or is switched off by booze. No matter what the reason, he inflicts great pain and suffering through uninhibited remarks and comments. Most times he will deeply regret such horrible words when sober – if he can remember them or if he is reminded of them. These same remarks tend to be repeated on the next drunken occasion, and the partner and other people affected may then feel that there has to be some truth in them because they have been regurgitated. In fact, it is because the remarks have gone into the drunken memory banks to be reiterated when he is in the same condition.

People with alcohol problems tend to go to enormous lengths to conceal the extent of the problem from their loved ones, extended family, workplace colleagues and friends. Sometimes they manage to conceal the fact that the drinking is out of hand for some considerable time, but more usually it is like the famous 'elephant in the room' syndrome: everybody knows about it yet no one is able, or perhaps willing, to confront it directly. As already discussed, the name of the elephant game is for the partner to take responsibility for the elephant's actions.

Ignorance of the existence of a problem

Although rare, it is not unknown for people to be admitted to treatment centres for alcohol dependence and for their partners to report that they were not aware of the existence of an alcohol problem at all, or of the extent of the problem. This may of course be a form of denial and a reluctance to face the issue, but it also reflects the devious skill of the individual who manages to hide the problem.

I remember meeting a lady in a treatment centre whose husband had 'dodged the column' for many years in that he skilfully avoided detection and treatment. He drank huge amounts of alcohol, increasing in volume and frequency over the years, almost exclusively in secret. As his dependency progressed he used all sorts of schemes and tricks to hide it from her, including the use of simple avoidance, eye drops, breath fresheners and even a face blusher.

This man had serious health and personal issues, of course. You cannot drink at that rate for that long and avoid having major medical and domestic problems. They were both very unhappy in their relationship, though she did not know why exactly, and she worried about his deteriorating physical condition over time. He would say to this day that he did not realize that his drinking was that significant, and he believed that it was even helping to improve their relationship. For example, sometimes when he drank they would have some form of personal intimacy together that was absent on other occasions.

This man had attended practically every medical specialist with all sorts of varied symptoms, and this particular aspect of his story is very common. I know that many people with alcohol problems are 'gloriously missed' by many healthcare professionals who treat them for what they think are problems that are unrelated to alcohol. The same thing applies to family members of alcoholics, who attend consultants for a wide variety of physical symptoms that are often actually stress-induced.

Most recently, this particular man had undergone investigations for neurological problems as he was regularly suffering from blinding and persistent headaches. His wife feared that he would die and was convinced that he must have a brain tumour. After the usual battery of tests, the neurologist could not find any physical cause for his headaches. He was extremely thorough, and I think he must have also been suspicious that this individual might have an alcohol problem. In any event he was keen to get to the source of the headaches. So he took a simple alcohol history (which none of the previous specialists had done) and asked the man firmly but respectfully to come clean with him about his drinking practices. This approach revealed the truth. On hearing the pattern and scale of the drinking, the doctor informed his patient, in no uncertain terms, that his problems were entirely due to his alcohol intake. He referred the man for alcohol counselling, and I am delighted to report that he suffered no further medical symptoms when he stopped drinking and has made a full recovery to date.

His wife was equally surprised with the 'new' diagnosis, and there were tears and anger. She felt she was stupid not to have realized that he had developed an alcohol problem, and for a period of time was consumed with a deep sense of shame that she had failed in her role, as she saw it, as his partner. With time they resolved many personal issues, and to this day they are happy together.

I wish that all problems were that simple.

Total denial by the partner is very rare. Most go through phases of uncertainty about whether or not the cause of their partner's problems is drinking.

Has he a problem or am I exaggerating?

He would eventually come home and collapse in a total heap on the sofa. I had to throw out new suites of furniture over two years because of the cigarette burns that he made when he was intoxicated. One night on holiday he got very drunk and came back to the apartment like a man who was utterly possessed. I tried to stop him coming into my room but he was too strong. My leg got trapped in the door and was badly hurt. He threatened suicide regularly to terrorize me. One day he stormed out of the house and sped away at about 90 miles per hour with his passport in his hand, yelling that I would never see him again. That night he came home violently sick and manic.

From this story it would seem obvious that this person's partner has an alcohol problem. Regrettably, this particular individual never got the specialist help he required and tragically died from drinking too much. However, his partner did receive help and made a new life for herself.

Partners sometimes do not ask for help because they don't know where to go, but often it is because they worry that they might be exaggerating the problem. Such thoughts often stop people from getting help until the situation is well established. As a general rule, the more the drinking behaviour is established or entrenched, the more difficult it is to change, or even to initiate change.

Partners also fear that they themselves might be the problem and are afraid they will be harshly judged if they ask for help. There tend to be common features in the development of alcohol problems from the partner's perspective. Typically, an alcohol-related incident occurs that is deeply upsetting for the partner. The drinker assures his partner that it will not happen again, and when it does he reassures her once again. She does not want to cause a fuss so she remains silent and puts up with it. Further events happen and excuses are offered and accepted. The pattern continues until there is a spiral of damage, resulting in the partner and family suffering to the point of apathy and inertia. She becomes resigned to her fate and no longer retains any hope of a decent peaceful existence.

The word 'spiral' is very appropriate in this context. Some writers have described addiction as a vortex or a whirlpool, and there is no doubt in my mind that the sense of being 'sucked down', whether gradually or quickly, is a good metaphor for addiction. The deteriorating spiral is familiar to anyone with alcohol problems, too. It works for the alcoholic, as Figure 2 shows.

The notion of 'rock bottom' comes from terms used within meetings of the self-help organization Alcoholics Anonymous. 'Personal rock bottom' implies that alcoholics may have to reach their own personal lowest point before starting recovery. Spiralling downwards is a progressive feature of addiction. It should be pointed out, though, that recovery is also progressive. Of course, each person is different and a unique personal spiral map could be drawn for everyone with an alcohol problem.

The spiral concept obviously also works for the partner. Over a period of time she too is dragged down into a whirling abyss by an emotional force and eventually 'drowns', without help, in a sea of aggressive emotional eddies.

This is also best depicted in diagram form; see Figure 3 overleaf.

She too can experience a 'personal rock bottom'. After a while she feels too embarrassed and ashamed to ask for help, because in her own mind she has allowed it to happen and she believes that she no longer has the authority or right to complain. If she does say something to him, she is likely to be met with a number of responses that may stall any possible progress, such as prevarication, denial and hostility. Sometimes the person with the alcohol dependency is compliant and assures her that he will stop or change, or uses further plausible excuses to justify the drinking: 'You know I have been under a lot of stress', for example. Sometimes the issue is thrown back at her: 'I wouldn't drink if it wasn't for you and your problems.'

In reality there are all sorts of fears and anxieties that prevent her from realizing properly what exactly is going on. She is often in fact

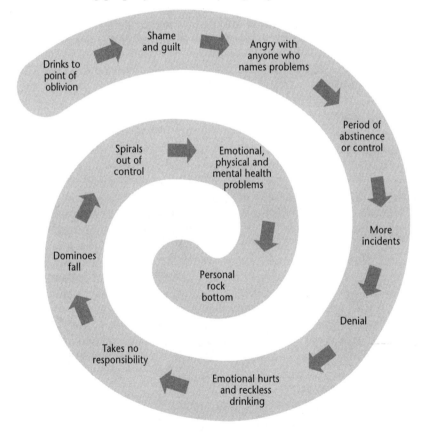

Figure 2 Spiral from the alcoholic's perspective

totally consumed by fear. What if he is indeed alcoholic? There is a fear of the diagnosis due to shame and guilt. The 'down-and-out' stereotype of the alcoholic is deep in her head. Stigma is still commonplace.

She tends to go over it all again and again in her mind. Maybe all he is saying is absolutely right: maybe I am ugly, stupid, boring, frigid, useless, etc. If I confront his issues, will he lose his job and will we have no money to live on? Will I lose my home if I complain? Was there a problem in our relationship prior to the drinking? When did it actually start? Did having children cause the problems? Should I have stopped working? Did I neglect my partner?

Denial may seem a better prospect when confronted with all these frightening, whirling, mostly internalized questions and emotions. So, terrified of any movement at all, she may decide 'better the devil you know'. All these circular sentiments go round inside her head and are

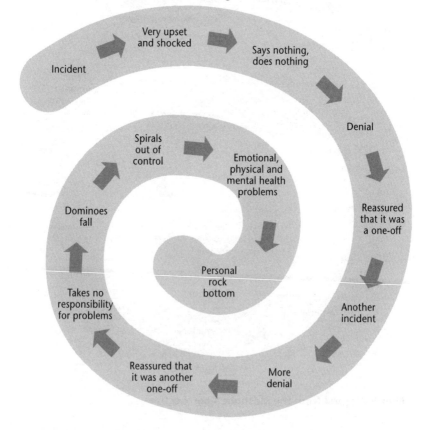

Figure 3 Spiral from the partner's perspective

seldom satisfactorily resolved. Indeed, it may seem that there is no solution. If she half-heartedly approaches someone for help, she may be disappointed with their advice.

She is faced with all sorts of simple and complex dilemmas too. If he asks for money, should she give it to him? Should she call the police when he is aggressive? Should she keep alcohol in the home? Will the children be badly hurt or irreparably damaged? Many of these worries are complicated in some cases by other forms of addictive behaviours, such as gambling, other drugs and obsessive–compulsive type behaviours – with pornography as just one example.

Checklist of possible signs of an alcohol problem, from the partner's perspective

Signs may include:

- being subjected to an out-of-character (other than when alcohol is involved) tirade of abusive language or aggression during or after a spell of drinking;
- the presence of increased lying, half-truths and deceptions;
- making excuses for his behaviour;
- hiding alcohol from him;
- trying to control the pace at which he drinks: watering down bottles, for example, buying less alcohol, pouring it down the sink;
- discovering watered-down bottles or alcohol in coffee or tea or soft drinks, or finding bottles, tins or cans around the house or in the garden;
- cancelling parties and other social events or commitments behind his back, for fear that he will drink at them;
- calling work to lie for him and saying that he has the flu, for example, after pay day or on a Monday morning or before a shift starts;
- awareness of a smell of alcohol from him, or other strong scent to mask it;
- awareness of his increasingly bad hygiene, neglect of his appearance and bed wetting or soiling;
- awareness of his secretive or furtive behaviour;
- strange phone calls that do not make sense to you or from people you don't know;
- a sense of shame or guilt because of his drinking;
- depression for you or for him;
- repeated drink-related incidents and fights;
- memory loss on his part after a period of drinking;

- sudden changes in his tolerance for alcohol; less alcohol seems to make him more drunk;
- periods of absence from home on his part;
- increasing unreliability and irrational behaviour on his part;
- personality changes and swift mood swings on his part;
- his heavy drinking;
- his binges or bouts;
- 'technology terrorism': being bombarded by abusive phone calls, texts or emails.

Of course, this checklist could be indicative of other problems and is certainly not exhaustive. Every problem drinker has individual signs and symptoms. In very simple terms, if you believe there is an alcohol problem, there is a problem. Be careful not to try to control his drinking by drinking with him or at his pace. This could lead to a development of alcohol problems for you and will also be ineffective in trying to control his drinking in the long term.

Trust your instincts!

In the vast majority of cases where alcohol problems occur in relationships, however, it is painfully obvious to the partner early on that an alcohol problem is present. In fact, many people become expert at detecting even the slightest hint that their partner is drinking. Most say that they know that he is drinking by the first word that comes out of his mouth when he comes home, or by some word or turn of phrase he uses while on the phone, or by a look or a mannerism, or indeed by the fact that there is no contact or avoidance of contact. Many live in dread and terror of what they are going to face when the drinker returns home, for example after a night on the town.

The absolute definitive diagnosis does not matter at this stage; what matters most is that you get the help you require. You deserve this help, but you may have to take that on trust too until your confidence and knowledge improve.

Is it my fault?

Inertia – an inability to move – and fear are made worse by the niggling fear or belief that what he is saying repeatedly is true. It is worth repeating that reluctance to get help involves the fear of being judged and the horrible feeling that it might indeed be 'my fault'. Remember, it will get worse if it is not addressed. You will need to recognize the problem. As the famous saying goes; 'You cannot change what you cannot see.'

Does his drinking and deterioration reflect failure on my part?

Most people who find themselves in a relationship with a problem drinker have a sense of shame and guilt. They will want to try to fix what is wrong without making it very public. This is based on the idea that 'I screwed up, so I should fix it.' This righting or fixing reflex is universal. Unfortunately, the focus at this stage is not on righting herself but rather on sorting out his problems in general and his drinking specifically. Her inability to fix him leads to that spiral of further guilt, shame and self-loathing. Remember, progressive deterioration is a feature of all addictions.

She is confronted regularly too by his rationalizations or excuses. He tells her that he drinks because she is stupid, or because she had let him down years ago or because she got pregnant or because she is no longer attractive to him or because she complains too much, and she sadly believes it and even internalizes that belief to the point that it may become a 'fixed delusion' that is difficult to shake off.

Her fears are made worse by real events that have happened in her own life. If there was childhood alcoholism in her own family of origin or other traumatic events in her life, she may feel she does not deserve any better or that she is not worthy of a good or reasonable relationship. In many cases this belief will be picked away at by her partner, who will use her feelings of inadequacy and insecurity to justify and excuse his own behaviours. In a sense, he feeds off her insecurity to make his own ego feel stronger.

How can I cope?

I have tried everything to make things better in our lives. I have been cross and I have been overly compliant. I have ignored abusive remarks and I have been silent. I have not commented at all, when he is drinking, on his behaviour. I have removed myself from the home. I have screamed at him, threatened him, bribed him, manipulated him, I have refused to sleep with him and I have slept with him when he is rotten with drink. We have had days of all sight and no talk. I have drunk with him. I have refused to drink with him. I have tried to reduce his intake, I have watered down alcohol in bottles so that he would be less drunk without him knowing, I have tried to restrict him to beer and wine instead of vodka and whiskey, I have locked him in the house and I have given him free rein to come and go as he pleases. Nothing has worked. Where do I go from here? I am going stark staring mad.

These are typical amalgamated comments from partners in the early days of help-seeking. The partner is completely frustrated in this state and survives with little hope of change for a better life.

Many partners suffer mild to severe forms of mental health issues: anxiety, panic attacks, stress, trauma, phobias and depression. They may also suffer from medical health problems such as psoriasis and other skin problems, high and low blood pressure, sleep disturbance, exhaustion, listlessness, and maybe also more serious conditions. We know that stress and tension can lead to major health problems. Living with alcoholism is often described as 'walking on eggshells', delicately trying to avoid emotional landmines that might set him off again. She is terrified that anything she might say or do could make him drink or lead to an argument that leads to more drink.

Here follows a selection of comments made by partners during counselling sessions that were intended to assess the possible issue of alcoholism at home and to help them cope with the problems:

- Am I mad because he totally denies that he is alcoholic?
- He drinks six pints every night. Does that mean that he is alcoholic? (Amounts on their own rarely are definitive in this regard, though obviously the more a person drinks the higher the risk. Therapists are far more interested in the impact of alcohol on the partner than in the amount.)
- If he is not alcoholic, what is wrong? Because I am subject to threatening behaviour and constant criticism.
- He takes money from my purse without my permission.
- The only way I can sleep is to have a knife under my pillow, in case he comes in and violently demands sex. I live in squalid terror.
- I find hidden bottles everywhere.
- He goes missing for days on end and never lets me know where he is. Last time he was gone for five days and I only discovered where he was when I saw a receipt for the hotel he was staying in.
- Can you get him to talk about personal issues that he has not disclosed? I am convinced that he has endured some deep personal trauma years ago.
- I only know when he has been drinking when he tries to compensate for his behaviour.
- I am so angry I could kill him.
- The main problem is the upset to the children.
- I know when he is very drunk because he comes home late at night and he has the telly or the music blaring.

- When we are out he never knows when to stop; it's so embarrassing.
- I miss the old person I used to know; his personality has changed utterly.
- He is always right – he 'yesses' me to death.
- My family have lost all interest in me because I have never followed through on making changes and so they are fed up with me. I have no support from them now.
- I want to leave him but what will happen if I go? Will he harm or kill himself?
- I bought a breathalyser and he knows he can't come in unless he passes the test. (She has become a surveillance expert. Another partner once told me that she video-recorded her husband when he was drunk, in the vain hope that it would help him to see what he was like. She hoped that he might change when he saw himself on video after sobering up.)
- His mood changes so quickly, for nothing that is apparent or obvious. One minute we are having a lovely evening and the next thing there is a horrible row, and it is often due to jealousy after a few drinks. He is like Dr Jekyll and Mr Hyde.
- The latest thing that happened has devastated me. When he was drunk the last time he kicked me. He was never violent before.
- We went away for a nice weekend to try to improve our relationship. He drank to the point of oblivion and I woke up to find him on top of me, thumping me in the middle of the night. He had no recollection of what happened the next day and even asked me what had happened to my face first thing in the morning.
- He can't let a day go by without referring to my issues from the past.
- You could be a lot worse.
- I feel sorry for him because he loves his wine.

Many partners will themselves turn to alcohol, other drugs and other addictive behaviours to try to cope. She erroneously thinks she can control the pace of his drinking by drinking with him. She may also feel it will stop her from feeling so low. But alcohol acts as a depressant, so people are likely to become more depressed and in danger of developing an addiction themselves. Benzodiazepines, sleeping tablets and even some over-the-counter medications, such as those containing codeine, may seem like a solution but only lead to more problems and still more complicated relationships.

Sexual problems

Living with a partner who has an alcohol problem almost inevitably means that there is some form of sexual problem. These range from performance anxiety to impotence and everything in between. Sexual problems result from drunken taunts such as 'You have no interest in sex so you must be a lesbian', 'You are useless in bed', 'You are thinking about your old boyfriend', and so on.

The truth is that being sexy or loving is very difficult, to say the least, if there is alcohol in the bedroom, because of

- exhaustion
- awful smell of body odour
- a bad smell of alcohol or stale alcohol on the breath
- wetting or soiling the bed
- jealousy and paranoia, accusations of infidelity
- an inability to get or sustain an erection
- hurtful comments
- clumsy manoeuvres, painful gropes or bites because of intoxication
- a history of infidelity or one-night stands
- an ongoing relationship on either side
- practical worries
- poor self-esteem.

Partners may be exposed to sexually transmitted illnesses (STIs) as a result of infidelities. One lady I saw was convinced by her husband that she must have contracted the infection somewhere herself; she subsequently sought and received treatment for it, even though he knew exactly where he had contracted the STI as the result of a drunken one-night stand.

One partner summed it all up like this for me;

Sex was almost non-existent; I did not want him near me. Fumbling at night only served to make me feel I was prostituting myself. Refusing him sex opened up other abuses. He would say that I was gay, I was frigid, I was surely having an affair, and most hurtfully, with no reason whatsoever, that I was sexually abused as a child by my father. How could I have sex with him in such circumstances and when there were no niceties? We had a marriage that lasted 40 minutes maximum every day.

Other issues

There are all sorts of other difficulties that can lead to problems in the relationship. The partner or the problem drinker or both can have 'co-morbid problems'. By this I mean they may have had a history of mental health problems, including treatment or not, for anxiety, depression or psychotic illnesses. There are also unusual situations which pose major complications, and some of these are mentioned in Chapter 6.

Partners too might have separate complications that require help. Many people, when they come for help about their partner's drinking, reveal important and upsetting previous occurrences in their own lives that have little relevance to their current partner. These distressing life events are often resurrected by the therapy itself, or perhaps because of a shadow from the past at a particular time. For example, some people deal with issues from their past because of some innocent remark made by their own child, or because of the very fact that they have children, or because the ages of their children revive old traumas. They realize, in retrospect, how vulnerable they were when they were that age.

Some people are attracted to their partners because they behave in very different ways from previous partners or family members. Unfortunately it is all too easy to be blinded by that specific fact, with the risk of harm in a different way if an alcohol problem is present. Sometimes people develop a relationship because the loved one is the opposite of their father or mother, where the parental relationship was traumatic. I am thinking, for example, of a number of people who were attracted to someone who seemed very gentle, and not physically violent like their own parent. Regrettably, people can be so focused on the absence of these traits that they fail to see the whole picture and later discover that there are other important character or personality flaws in their partners that cause major difficulties.

One such woman described it like this:

He was never physically violent in any way when we went out together before we were married. I loved this aspect of him and thought he was so considerate, mannerly and gentle. Later on the drinking kicked in. His pattern was to stay out most of the night and sleep during the day. He had only sporadic contact with everyone else. He could not cope with any criticism or even a hint of criticism. He could be verbally abusive but only when very drunk. He was mostly uncommunicative and silent in a sulky way. He thinks I am a crusader who wants to rid alcohol from the world. Actually, all I ever wanted was to have a peaceful normal life.

Another partner said:

He warned me when he was drunk that there was a darker side to him that might emerge if I pushed him hard enough. He used to repeat that every time he was drunk, and sometimes would shout it over and over again when standing inches from my face.

Another person told me that the person she married, who she thought was non-violent, later developed an aggressive side when the drinking pattern was well established:

The hardest thing to cope with was the rapid changes in his personality. He would be the life and soul of the party when we would be out, then would change for no apparent reason (apart from alcohol!) on the way home and I knew I would be in for it. He would go purple with rage and I was subject to dreadful beatings. My heart is broken; the way he has behaved is despicable.

Interestingly, she said that this side of his personality emerged when he had increasing responsibilities: his problems developed when they had children together.

Of course, we have already established that physical violence is not the only way to be hurt when living with someone who has an alcohol problem. Words, silence and actions can also be very violent. Silence is a sharp weapon in relationship difficulties. In alcoholic relationships this method is, like many other issues in addiction, taken to the extreme.

A young woman in her thirties:

After a drunken row, which he typically could not remember, he would treat me with frosty silence. It was not just for a few hours but would go on for a week or longer, or even more if he continued to drink. He knew exactly what he was doing; he would not make eye contact with me, and the children would be included in this rebuke though they did nothing wrong. Sometimes, to add to the hurt, he would sleep in his office and not come home at all. I at least had stood up for myself when he was drunk. We would both be miserable and somehow it would end usually by me apologizing for something I did not do!

I want to finish this chapter on a positive note. Couples recover and get well. It happens every day of the week:

I gave him an ultimatum and that time I actually meant it – and, more importantly, he knew that I meant it: if he did not go for treatment I was gone. He went in and we have never been happier together. Over ten years since he took that step, and I ask myself why I did not insist earlier. When he was working on the 12-step programme and I was going to Al-Anon it was the best period of our lives together. He was sober, not just dry, and back to himself. He was completely clean and did not use hash. He was gentle and sensitive. I did work on myself and got rid of the hurt and resentment. We even had a family in that time and were very happy together.

Frequently asked questions

My wife has an alcohol problem but does not accept it. I firmly believe that I am right in the arguments we have and I fail to see any other side. The therapist said that I am 'sincerely deluded'.

There is no point in arguing with someone who is drunk. Obviously one would need to know a lot more about your circumstances and history, but the role of counselling is not to be some sort of emotional referee to decide who is right and wrong and then dish out rewards and punishments. The counsellor tries to see every side of the equation. There is a quote that I love and it goes like this: 'There are three sorts of people in the world, those that can count and those that can't.' Whatever anyone else feels about that, there are at least three sides to consider in every marital situation: your side, your partner's side and the truth. It is probably even more complicated than this, because there are all sorts of different perceptions of what constitutes the truth. It is probably a universal truth in all domestic rows that each party feels justified in his or her own particular stance. In relationship counselling, most participants make the mistake of trying to change their partner exclusively, and do not focus enough on their own required changes. A subtle change in this direction can paradoxically bring helpful results if both parties focus on their own change requirements.

'Sincerely deluded' is an old catchphrase in this field (I will come back to it in Chapter 5). It usually refers to the alcoholic who is in abject denial. He does not accept that he has a problem, and sincerely holds this view. Partners can be sincerely deluded too if this definition is used. Do discuss all this with your therapist.

Sometimes I think it's easier and maybe even better not to complain when he is drinking. When I make a fuss about his drinking there is hell to pay.

I am not sure if it is in fact easier, except perhaps in the very short term. If your partner is getting drunk regularly at home or coming home drunk, then there are inevitably going to be major problems to contend with and sadly a price for you to pay. It would be nigh on impossible to ignore that problem on a regular basis. I know what you mean, though, and challenging someone with an alcohol problem in whatever way, even if it is most sensitively handled, may lead to outpourings of anger and distress. Many partners pretend to be asleep, so to speak, and hope it passes without desperate disruption for the whole family. In the long term, though, this cannot be the right way to deal with this as you are, in effect, taking on huge responsibility for behaviour that is not caused by you yourself. Not causing a dispute and staying silent about an unpleasant occurrence is very hard to do. It seems to me that it places an unbearable burden on the partner and is almost a prescription for emotional and health problems if it is on a prolonged basis. Above all else, you need to make sure you protect yourself if there is any form of violence. Talking to your partner should take place when he is sober, but you may be met with denial or forget-fulness. Counselling and self-help groups can help you to handle such matters in a more thought-out manner, but it certainly will take time to get results.

4

'Enabling' and survival
How partners cope

This chapter is principally about the partner or the nearest and dearest. However, it also relates in many ways to other family members who are living with alcohol problems, such as the parents, children and siblings of alcoholics.

> My husband is a shocking drunk. He is by far the most negative person I ever met and when I think back he was like that when I first started going out with him. Why did I marry him and why did I stay there? I don't honestly know – I ask myself these questions every day of my miserable life with him. I suppose I thought or maybe even believed I might be able to change him, but that was obviously impossible and he got worse and worse. He was and is always cruel to me. He treats me with utter disdain. He is no longer capable of physical violence, though I am, and I regret that sometimes I take out my frustrations on him. He sits in the same chair in the sitting room, day in and day out, and orders alcohol by phone and has it delivered by taxi if I'm not around. I am utterly resigned to my way of life and I don't even try to stop him drinking these days. He has a terrible heart condition too, so to be really honest I am just waiting and hoping that he will die soon. My grown-up children hate him and will never call at the house when he is around. I get on with my own life as best as I possibly can.

Sad to think family situations become as entrenched and bitter as this, isn't it? Most cases are thankfully not as extreme as this tale related to me by a 65-year-old lady. Clearly this person had coped with enough problems and decided to manage as well as possible on a day-to-day basis.

Chapter 6 discusses what might be called Machiavellian dynamics within families of alcoholics, where, as with the story above, actions and reactions are more complex. However, most family members do their level best to help and support their loved one, and wish and hope that the problem will be resolved as soon as possible. They bend over backwards to make things right and to avoid any perceived or possible threats to a normal peaceful life.

Easier said than done!

How on earth do you cope with such a devastating ongoing problem as described above? It is so facile to give trite advice and simple instructions, but very difficult to take action when the pressure is on. Alcoholic family dramas defy ordinary logic.

There is a lot of jargon used by therapists and treatment centres. Some terms have come to be accepted without any rigorous examination of their truth or practical relevance. In the treatment arena and in literature, much has been spoken and written about the terms 'denial', 'enabling', 'co-dependence' and 'tough love'. They have been used extensively to describe family responses to alcohol problems, and each deserves some serious attention and debate in its own right. For those living in intimate proximity to alcoholism, these words have served, in certain circumstances, to make matters worse for family members who are trying to survive. These clichéd concepts can be used or interpreted to further stigmatize and traumatize people who in most cases are simply struggling to cope and make sense of their situation.

Denial

Denial has been mentioned several times and cannot be ignored in any discussion about addictive substances or behaviours. Denial is said to occur when family members, or the problem drinker herself, refuses or is unable to admit or recognize the reality of the situation – the reality being, of course, that alcohol is causing the individual and her family serious health, social, financial, emotional, practical and mental health problems.

Alcohol problems do not exist in a vacuum, though, and people have other unrelated serious illnesses, their own particular personalities and life events that all add to the mix. The 'alcoholic' is also in relationships with people who have other issues, life events and personalities, which are all unique to those individuals and which again add to the cocktail that makes up any relationship. Indeed, most of these factors pre-date the development of the alcohol problem.

Rooting out denial is thought to be essential to successful recovery, and it is hard to argue otherwise. 'You can't change what you can't see', as already noted, is the oft-repeated mantra in this field, and again this is true, but how do you get to see it clearly and then is it really that simple? Recognizing alcohol dependence is difficult for even the most trained eye and there is little science available to help in making a definitive diagnosis. There exists no absolute biological test to demonstrate the presence or absence of alcohol dependence. Like many other aspects surrounding the complex story of alcoholism, it is just not that easy to recognize. Sometimes when you are so close to somebody or something you cannot see exactly what is going on. If you stand back and have another look from a different angle, you can often get a much better perspective.

Denial is a feature of alcoholism, as it is in every form of addiction. It is a feature in many other areas of ordinary life too, however.

People may deny:

- their own sexuality – being gay, for example;
- being depressed or anxious, being sad;
- being stressed and unable to cope;
- getting older, losing faculties;
- having a tremor or shake;
- discovering a lump;
- the inevitability of death;
- the paucity or strength of their relationships, and problems within a relationship or within a marriage – that their partner is having an affair, for example;
- their own personal history;
- sexual abuse and many other traumatic events from the past;
- increasing debt;
- powerlessness; and much more.

Denial is not therefore solely confined to the field of addiction. Indeed, social mores and constraints encourage denial. We all want to present ourselves in a good light to our families, communities and the broader society. 'How are you?' is usually greeted with 'Fine' – a *fine* example of denial in many cases! Imagine this response to the question 'How are you?' in a social setting such as the supermarket:

> Actually I feel really bad. My wife is drinking obnoxiously and my life is falling apart. I know I should separate but I am too frightened to do so because I am afraid I will not have enough money to cope. She beat me up last night and we haven't had sex for three years. I am so ashamed of the failure in our marriage but I will stay for the children's sake.

For most people in such social circumstances, it is understandable and far less complicated to simply reply, 'I'm fine.' The trouble is, people get so used to this pernicious normalized form of denial that it still operates in other settings, such as a visit to the GP, where the individual can reply 'I'm fine' as a tried and automatic response and in so doing misses out on another opportunity for help.

Denial is functional as well. It is natural to deny reality if reality is unpalatable or unacceptable. For example, few people are instantly able to accept that their relationship or marriage is over or that their partner is doomed to failure. Denial is probably progressive in most cases. As a general rule, the greater the investment the individual puts into the relationship, the greater the denial when things start to break down.

Denial is not even a constant in the history of someone's drinking problems. People with alcohol problems go in and out of denial at different times, in different circumstances and to varying degrees. Sometimes it is clear and obvious to someone that alcohol is the problem, while at other times it is not that evident. Situations do deteriorate over time but subtle changes are hard to see and quantify as they occur. Periods of relative calm can convince people, and especially loved ones, that the problems are due to something else. 'Maybe it *is* my fault', for example, because 'when I am nice to her she does not drink as much'. Maybe the problem is depression or maybe 'he is under too much pressure at work'.

Enabling

'Enabling' is another hackneyed word in this arena, but one that is rarely analysed or understood properly. It is bandied about willy-nilly in the treatment field and, like 'denial', can be used to demonize partners of alcoholics. You can attend wonderful courses to gain insight into enabling. If you are enabling the alcoholic it is implied that you are doing something wrong, and that you are in fact contributing to the problem or maybe even causing it. A discussion about enabling begs the following questions: is there a right way to manage someone with an alcohol problem? Is there a manual for partners to read that might help them cope? No and no would be my responses to these questions.

The word itself, according to the dictionary definition, actually implies somebody being helpful and facilitative, but in addiction treatment it has come to indicate a failure on the part of the partner or other family members to deal effectively with, say, his wife's drinking. Therefore, he is actively facilitating her denial of the problem, and therefore once again it may be implied that he is at fault to a greater or lesser extent for her drinking.

In some of the literature, the advice is to stop nagging and to facilitate your partner's drinking. When she comes home drunk, for example, you should treat her with kindness. She comes in at 3.30 in the morning, shouting and arguing and using foul and abusive language. She demands food and more drink. She is volatile. At one and the same time she is loving and sloppy and aggressive and hostile. In these circumstances, should you sit back and say nothing? It is a very tall order, and what message does it give? You are in effect saying: 'No matter how you treat me, I will accept it.' For safety's sake in some cases you should not be there, or should get out of that situation, but again it is just not that easy. Should you abandon the children? Why should you leave your own home?

One woman told me that she would never be violent if her husband simply did not nag when she comes home drunk. 'Why can't he just leave me alone when I'm drunk?' she said, because, if he did, 'I would not respond with violence.' Is this denial at work too? This famous (or infamous) nugget of illogical wisdom still holds popular belief. It means that alcohol is not a factor in the violence at all, nor in her partner's anxiety or worry about her behaviour all evening. It does not even properly consider his fear or powerlessness.

Typical examples of 'enabling' are paying her drinking debts, covering up for her in work or social situations, picking her up after she falls down, and so on. Yet many of these behaviours are functional for the greater good of the whole family system, and in some circumstances life-saving. Enabling, as it has been defined, may only be a natural response to living with unacceptable behaviour. Gradually over time people accept their lot and have no sense of hope or the ability, without help, to move in any direction. Family members are often stuck in a type of emotional jail. They try hard to ignore (deny) their circumstances. Partners have great difficulty seeing the wood for the trees and are frozen in a pattern of behaviour that is based only on short-term results.

Brinkmanship (should that be, to coin a word, 'drinkmanship'?) is common. Partners will often make wild threats in the heat of the battle that are never likely to be carried out:

- I'll give you one last chance.
- If that happens again I will definitely leave you.
- I will tell your own family.
- I will take the children from you and emigrate.
- I will take you to court.
- I am going home to my mother with the children.

Of course, a verbal threat is not worth the paper it is written on! Partners should always be advised never to make idle threats. Such threats usually only serve to further undermine their confidence and to reaffirm a sense of powerlessness to make positive changes in their lives. Sometimes they feel honour bound to follow through on a threat, but it only makes circumstances worse because it was ill conceived or poorly thought through. Once again, talk is cheap.

Co-dependence

'Co-dependency' is another term that has been written about extensively and has helped many people. Unfortunately it has sometimes added to a sense of confusion and guilt. It is responsible for copious writing and was probably made most famous by the author Melody Beattie in her excellent book *Codependent No More*. It has been used in conjunction, and almost interchangeably, with 'enabling'. Some writers have even called co-dependency a disease in itself and another form of addiction. It indicates that the partner is dependent on someone who is dependent, in order to resolve his own unresolved needs. The partner in co-dependence therefore 'loves too much' or is 'too stupid' or 'too lacking in insight' to get out of the situation. He is, in short, addicted to her and her behaviour. He sees his role as to be responsible for her behaviour, and his own needs and wants are subsumed into whatever she wants. He reacts and responds almost exclusively to her behaviour. He is typically the son of an alcoholic himself and 'attracted' to the mayhem that is alcoholism. He is a fixer. He does not have much of a life of his own.

Here it should be noted that the argument has become somewhat sexist, and co-dependence has been mostly used to describe female partners. Many writers on the subject, in my opinion, take little account of practical explanations for women's plight living with alcoholism. Women still occupy an inferior role in most societies. They are principally responsible for the children. Except in the higher socio-economic groups, women are still largely dependent on their partner's income. Does that fact alone contribute to co-dependence? I would say it certainly does.

Men, of course, are also co-dependent, as defined. They are often ashamed to admit that they have no control over their partner's drinking or behaviour.

Please do not get me wrong: to repeat, the term 'co-dependence' and its implications have helped many people, men and women, to realize their situation and to take steps to improve their particular circumstances. However, there are intricate issues in play and they need to be teased out carefully and handled with great sensitivity in therapy if partners are not to be further victimized and traumatized by therapists and treatment staff with only a modicum of understanding of addiction.

Doctors, social workers and counsellors can all be enablers, in denial and co-dependent too. Governments could be considered to be co-dependent on the drinks industry and the drinks industry co-dependent on its customers! Might treatment centres be considered to be co-dependent on their clients?

Tough love

Finally, among famous terms which are used to help partners and which may have developed in another less helpful direction, is 'tough love'. I suppose there are two extremes to managing traumatic situations: smother them with kindness on the one hand, and tough love on the other. As opposed to the gentler methods on the softer side of this divide, many people in Al-Anon and some therapists espouse the idea of tough love as a way to survive as a partner in alcoholism and to succeed in 'getting them sober'. Tough love means taking a hard line. No more 'enabling'. So it goes: you should detach from the problem behaviour, not from the person who is abusing alcohol. In the extremes of this method of coping or policy, there is no lying for the individual alcoholic and no covering up, no excuses offered for her behaviour and no going out with her to social functions or bars. She can make her own calls to excuse herself from work when she is hung over, she can make her own apologies to friends and family members she has offended, and she can pay for her own mistakes. In effect, in this approach as the partner, you live a separate life within the relationship in the hope or belief that some day she will stop drinking or some day she will agree to go in for treatment.

This assumes that she is indeed able to stop and will want to stop, and that treatment will be successful. As the partner, you develop your own interests and your own set of friends and you get on with life as best you can. Tough love means leaving her wherever she falls, not letting her in if she loses her keys, not cooking for her and not tidying up for her or cleaning her up, and lots more besides. All very well in theory but very difficult to implement and to carry through. What about the children in this approach, and what about your own needs for a satisfying, meaningful relationship? Are they just put on the back burner while you adopt a particular approach and wait until things change? Don't forget, things might never change for your partner.

Many partners tend to pin all their hopes on some form of treatment as being the only solution and yet, sadly, numerous problem drinkers never make it to formal treatment. Those that do manage to access treatment facilities may also unfortunately fail to get better. There are high relapse rates. Most people who stop drinking do so without professional help.

Whistle-blowing is a common feature of tough love. The person who is operating a tough love approach will not shirk any opportunity to call in the fact that his partner is drinking in a problematical way. Rather than using manipulative behaviour to influence or change the situation he will be direct in his communication. He will have no hesitation in ringing the police if she is drinking and driving. Tough love means that you have your own escape route – and she has, too, but will not take it. Using tough love, the partner decides that he will not be dominated by guilt or shame.

Tough love is hard to maintain, but of course has a lot of merit. Many partners need help to learn to love themselves before they take on such a difficult role. Tough love was, in part, the rationale for some practices in treatment centres years ago that we now consider to have been barbaric.

I like the work of Alex Capello and his co-workers in Birmingham. They have done extensive research but avoid terms such as 'co-dependence' and 'enabling' and instead talk of coping styles that partners adopt to survive in the face of drug and alcohol problems.

Staying there

Why do people stay in relationships where few or none of their needs are apparently being met? This is the six-million-dollar question that is debated over and over again.

Well, in simple terms there are many possible reasons why partners stay there. They may not believe that they deserve any better or they may be too frozen with fear or anxiety or too beaten down emotionally to have the strength to begin the process of change. They may see no possible escape from their circumstances and are perhaps like a condemned rabbit on a lonely road with an oncoming truck, mesmerized by the headlights and unable to get out of the way. Financial considerations and practical realities often keep them there too. Their drinking partner may have some hold over them. Blackmail and threats may be used against them: 'If you leave me I will tell your secrets', 'You will never be able to manage without me; you will never make anything out of yourself', 'You have no earning potential.' In recessionary times it is probably even harder to get out of a bad relationship because you are stuck there through economic necessity.

It is not unusual to meet people who feel obliged to stay in the relationship because their partner knows some 'dirty' personal secret about them. Members of their family of origin may have told them that they have made their bed so now must sleep on it, and thus they may have become isolated from sources of help and support. They may believe their partner's jibe that 'You drove me to drink.' They may also be in love with their partner still and hope against hope that things will somehow return to some form of normality. Fairytale or romantic love is still there in abundance. People respect their commitments to each other. No one likes to admit that the relationship has failed.

A man summed up 'staying there' for me when I was writing this book. He said that alcoholics do not take partners in marriage: rather, they take hostages. This gentleman had been married to his wife for over 20 years; both of them had significant alcohol problems when I met them, and a history of mental health worries including depression. The man had been sober for three years or more by the time he spoke to me, but his wife had had several failed attempts at treatment. They were now eventually in the throes of a legal separation. It was very sad for them both to have to admit failure after many years of happiness together and a number of children, who were still dependent on them.

A professional person with a medical background, this man described himself as suffering from 'Stockholm syndrome', a term coined after a robbery in a district in Stockholm in 1973 where hostages were taken. During their six-day ordeal, some of the victims became emotionally attached to their captors and even supported or defended them later when interviewed by the media and the police. Thus a new syndrome was created. There are several aspects of this syndrome that relate to someone living with alcohol problems. Perceptions in a hostage situation are all-important and are dominated by fear, captivity and isolation. The hostages believe that they will not survive and that the captors are willing to carry out the threats that are so obvious and frightening. In addition, they have no belief that they can escape. If you are taken hostage with your child, for example, escape seems futile anyway unless you can bring that child with you. In such situations the captor is focused on control and the hostage on survival. Any form of kindness is exaggerated in such rarefied situations.

I had of course heard of this before. In the context of living with alcohol problems it makes a great deal of sense. Compare it with the situation of the partner of an alcoholic who suffers all sorts of indignities but then finds his partner in tears, profoundly distressed at her own behaviour and assuring him that such an incident will not recur. Seeing the show of goodness and genuine remorse keeps him there, in the possibly false hope that his circumstances will dramatically change and revert to 'normal'.

Frequently asked questions

You sound dismissive of some the common terms used in this field and yet I feel strongly that my life was transformed when I stopped enabling my wife, and I feel the turning point for me was the use of tough love.

Well, I suppose I am a little dismissive of some of these terms, but my intention and goal is to help people to analyse critically such language in order to gain more practical help from it. I think the terms can be used positively or negatively. Partners should not be completely 'sold' them without having an opportunity to appraise them critically. Many people living with alcohol problems are half or part aware of terms such as 'enabling' and 'co-dependence' and are very self-critical as a result, taking on an extra sense of failure. Coping with alcohol problems as a partner is once again not easy, and there are practical reasons and realities that explain why people get stuck into co-dependence other than the well-established psychological or emotional explanations.

Insight is a wonderful thing, and many people gain insight by having an opportunity to really examine such terms, and to use the literature and discussion with other people to tease out meaning and practical applications of such issues. Clearly, in your own case this has been most beneficial, and of course that is great news for you. One size does not fit all, though, and people make progress at their own time and pace in such matters.

Although my wife has stopped drinking for the past four or five months and things are much more peaceful in our home, she is incredibly moody and irritable. She tells me she did it for me.

This is probably a case of a 'dry drunk', though this concept is also very controversial and not based on any real science. The idea is that someone stops drinking for the 'wrong' reason. It is said in treatment circles that in order for the individual alcoholic to be happy and content, she needs to accept her condition and stop because she wants to rather than because she needs or is forced to stop. There is always an element, however, of stopping for someone else's sake. As you indicated in your statement, in this case she stopped for your sake, and as a result there is probably a lot of resentment involved. Therefore she is all out of sorts and unhappy with her lot. This issue need to be carefully handled in joint sessions with a therapist. Of course, there may be other factors at work too. She could be suffering some other form of mental health problem or you yourself may need to examine your own attitudes to her.

5

Suffer the children

The plight of children in alcoholic homes must be covered, not just because it needs to be highlighted but also because it is a major part of the suffering of partners.

> When I was 11, I used to hear my mother being beaten up regularly in her bedroom by my drunken father. It was a nightly occurrence, or so it seemed, for ages and ages. I clearly remember putting my fingers in my ears, pulling the blanket over my head and singing to myself quietly in an attempt to block out the noise. I would not be able to stop crying.

A patient in her thirties, at that stage in an abusive relationship herself and drinking too much for her own good, told me this story. The long-term emotional damage inflicted on her by this abuse was profound.

Some children, tragically, are damaged before birth as a result of foetal alcohol syndrome, which may result from drinking during pregnancy. Symptoms range from mild hyperactivity to physical and mental damage.

One of the saddest things I hear in my work from people – both mothers and fathers – who have well-established alcohol problems is their strongly held conviction that their children are not adversely affected by their drinking. They *believe* this to be so before they get help, or perhaps they fool themselves into believing that there is no resultant harm. Regrettably, this is yet another understandable aspect of denial. It is a most unpalatable truth for parents to know and accept that their children are indeed damaged, emotionally, physically and psychologically, in their own homes by the drinking of their own parent or a parent's partner.

The vast majority of people with alcohol problems do care deeply about their children, of course, but nevertheless neglect or harm them through their drinking. That is not to say that children do not recover, as most of them do in fact make excellent recoveries. Healing is obviously much more likely if both parents make positive changes too.

To have it suggested that drinking is adversely affecting your child is deeply wounding and hard to come to terms with. The impact of drinking by a parent on children is always damaging to their emotional stability, certainly at the very least in the short term, and tragically this may continue throughout their lives. It can affect their very view of life, their mood and personalities and even their choice of partner. It can result in hospitalizations for medical and psychiatric problems. It can destroy their ability to start or maintain relationships. Without proper help, many go on to develop alcohol or drug problems and other addictive behaviours.

Managing the children well and informing them fully about the problem is a serious piece of work for the individual alcoholic and his partner. These matters need to be carefully and sensitively handled by both parents to avoid future problems.

One summer some years back when I was working abroad, training doctors in motivational interviewing and alcohol problems, I interviewed an in-patient in a local hospital who had just finished drying out (detoxification). He was still a little shaky physically but very kindly agreed to be interviewed in front of some 20 GPs in training. In the course of a wide-ranging interview he told me that his children were not affected at all by his drinking. He was emphatic about this. He had previously admitted to a recent consumption of two to three bottles of spirits per day and freely accepted that his alcohol dependence had been the dominating factor in his life for many years. When pushed on the reasons why he could claim that his children were not affected in any way by his drinking or by his behaviour when drinking, he replied, 'Because I never see them.'

Such a response would be funny if it were not so serious. It was true that he very rarely saw his children. He would come home drunk in the morning, sleep it off to some extent during the day, and then go out and drink all over again. He played no active part in their lives. 'I never see them' is such an honest reply and so common to people with alcohol problems.

I wanted to demonstrate a teaching point (never use sarcasm!) for the trainees, so I said, 'Congratulations: you are the first alcoholic I have ever met who has not adversely affected his children when actively drinking.' He simply thanked me, as he truly believed this to be the case. His responses are examples of 'sincere delusions' which are common in families with alcohol problems. He is self-deluded, but the belief is nonetheless sincerely held.

He also told us all that one of his daughters was training to be a health professional and that he was very proud of her. He told us that she had said many times to him that when she was fully qualified he would be one of her first patients and she would make him better from his 'drink problem'! So, of course, she was well aware of his situation and no doubt suffered from his drinking and his absences.

'What you don't see can't hurt you.' So it is said, but it is not true with regard to alcohol problems. It is simply impossible to hide alcohol problems or most of the consequences from children of every age within the home. They witness all sorts of events. They see and hear things they should not see or hear. They sense atmospheres, stress and unhappiness. People 'talk' loudly when drinking, even though they may not think they do. Even if the children do not see the actual events they sense hurt, pain, anxiety and fear. They often pick up tension from the non-drinking partner too. While younger children might not know specific details or the precise cause of problems, they intuitively know that something is wrong and react accordingly with distress.

Institutionalized abuse of children

The Ryan and Murphy reports on abuse in residential facilities run by the Roman Catholic Church in Ireland, published in 2009, revealed a scale of systemic, institutionalized abuse of children that shocked all right-minded people. The reports contained graphic chilling accounts of emotional, verbal, physical and sexual abuse inflicted on the most vulnerable children in our society. Media accounts of the long-term impact of such abuse on children were equally harrowing. Children of survivors talked of their loved ones being ripped apart, of destroyed personalities and of depression, mental health problems, addiction, attempted suicides and suicides.

All these reported events are very relevant to the various forms of abuse of children caused by alcohol. Living in the home of an active alcoholic might mean a 'sentence' of 10–18 years in a type of emotional prison, for which they have committed no crime. This shocking reality has received sparse attention. On a daily basis, numerous children are abused in private homes within family units where alcohol problems are acted out. The impact on children in such circumstances is of course less public and has not been the subject of any state-run inquiry to date. Such abuse is harder to detect but nonetheless damaging to their health, welfare and self-esteem. The likely future impacts on children are usually long-lasting, without help, and sadly are crippling in many cases. Their hidden turmoil interferes in all aspects of their lives and is hard to put accurately in words or to describe adequately. In a very real sense each child's suffering is unique and therefore impacts uniquely on that child's development, personality and life choices.

The desperate situation of children in such circumstances has been largely neglected. Services for children are woefully inadequate in this regard. In recent years, however, a little more has been written about children in alcoholic homes and a great deal explained about the short- and long-term impact of alcohol problems and alcohol dependence on children. Alcohol and addiction counsellors familiar with the trauma inflicted on children by alcohol abuse are all too aware of the way such trauma is presented in counselling when these children become adults.

In fact, much of the previous abuse is triggered when such people have children themselves and realize their own absolute vulnerability in retrospect. While those of us working in this field know about the patterns and consequences of abuse, children living with alcoholism rarely get the amount of support or help that they require. To this day they continue to get little or no assistance, back-up or information on coping with alcohol problems. It seems the general children's services are swamped and overloaded.

Unfortunately, too, even the specialist services are found wanting with regard to supporting children from alcoholic homes. Many treatment centres for alcohol problems are failing to respond to the needs of children. Most treatment centres, in my experience, do not adequately attend to their suffering. While many claim to run 'family' programmes, including family days, in practice children are usually vir-tually ignored. Rarely are young children consulted or indeed protected from the abuse that occurs in homes where alcohol is a problem. Even older children in their late teens are sometimes excluded from discus-sions. There is probably an unofficial age cut-off point for interviewing the children of alcoholics in these centres and hospitals because staff members are inadequately trained and therefore fearful of talking to younger children.

This is indeed a skilled area, and children's issues have to be handled very sensitively, but they should not be excluded or ignored. There is also insufficient liaison with child psychological and support agencies by the specialized treatment facilities. In certain regions, centres do not even have adequate written policies on mandatory reporting.

Resources are skimpy or non-existent. Some childcare services only operate in office hours! Did you know that family crises in relation to alcohol problems only occur in office hours? Of course, they are far more likely to occur later in the day and night, and typically some time after the pubs close.

Sadly, too, the child protection services often swing into action only *after* a serious event has taken place and therefore much emotional damage has already been done. Indeed, I would argue that ideally all children within active 'alcoholic' homes should have some form of child protection assessment and should certainly receive some help and support if the problem becomes known to health professionals. A lot of good could be done by simply explaining some aspects of alcoholism to children in an age-appropriate way, and of course by stating explicitly that they are not responsible for their parent's drinking. Children, like partners, often carry internalized guilt that their parent's drinking might, in some way, be caused by them.

I remember one case that throws the whole issue of child protection in this area into light. I was interviewing two children together. I did not instigate this interview: the children did! They asked for an appointment as their mother was known to me. The social services had not been involved, until they were informed, following the interview with the children, of their hapless and hopeless circumstances.

Their story goes as follows: their father had died years previously and their mother was attending an after-care programme sporadically, following on from in-patient treatment for alcoholism. Regrettably, the treatment was completely unsuccessful and she was drinking again in a desperately self-destructive manner. She would, for example, be found wandering the streets half-dressed and would invite strangers, mostly men from the pub, home for drinking binges. She would go out without locking the door. She was aggressive to the children, who lived with her, and would lash out at them, physically and verbally. She lived in a 'respectable' area. I have to admit to utter shock, despite some knowledge of the case, when her pre-teen daughter asked if I could please arrange for her and her younger brother to be taken into care. Such a blunt request! They were living in constant fear and suffering all sorts of hurts and indignities. For example, her mother used to spit in their faces when drunk. The daughter told me, in such an adult way, that their lives were completely miserable. This child showed incredible maturity born out of fear and desperation. She was old before her time. This is often a feature of the harm done by alcohol: it robs children of their natural youthful innocence and exuberance.

One more instance might illustrate the type of suffering endured by such children. Another child rang one day to ask me to admit his father to hospital. I knew his father well as he had completed an in-patient programme once before. I did not know the exact age of the child but knew he was very young because of the youth in his voice, though he was so grown up in his conversation. I discovered later that he was all of seven years of age, yet prior to ringing me he had arranged to activate his father's health insurance by calling the insurance company, he had tried to ring the family doctor and he had fed his baby sister. He proudly told me that he had cooked her beans on toast! He had also called the ambulance for his dad, who was 'not wake-able' (drunk) on the floor.

So how on earth can I do justice to the extent of damage and suffering that is actually inflicted on children when they live with problem drinking? There are a million different aspects that could be written about, and there are several complicating factors that might alleviate or exacerbate suffering. For example, if both parents are actively drinking there is no countervailing force or support and little hope for respite. Much damage is created, I believe, by the absence of a solid, consistent father or mother figure, especially in the younger years of growing up.

A young woman wrote for me in therapy:

> My father was alcoholic but he was not aggressive. In our home the harm that was done to me was caused by my mother. She was a vindictive woman who never got over the bitterness of their separation when I was in my early teens. I know now that she was overwhelmed with grief and anger, but she had problems all of her own. She used to line us up for beatings if one of us did anything wrong. I was verbally abused from a very young age, I think now it was because I was the spit of my father. I was told: 'Everyone knows what you are like', 'You are a bitch, a trollop', 'You will never amount to anything', 'You are ugly', 'Cry if you want, crying won't do you any good', over and over again. She would do bizarre things like turning off the heating and pretending that she had no oil to demonstrate another example of our father's neglect of us all. She would wail at night-time years after he had left about all the faults he had, and me and my siblings used to pray that she would get help for herself. She refused to allow us to have any contact with him. It was terrible living in that home with her, growing up.

Sometimes the non-drinking partner is so traumatized that she causes more problems for the children. She is cranky, tired, worried, insecure, frightened and irritable. As a result she is not as tuned in to the children's needs as she would otherwise be. Partners in this situation may respond in three extreme ways as a result. They can take all their frustrations out on the children, they can over-protect them or they can ignore them.

The health of the non-drinking partner may contribute to the problems for the children, too. She is hassled, depressed and anxious, and of course has her own personality issues and difficulties managing the situation. She can take out such anger, tiredness and frustration on the children. The children may be frustrated and upset with the non-drinking partner for doing nothing to prevent the hurt. They often feel compelled to take sides.

> I took your side in the battle against Dad and hated him always for his drinking. I could never understand why you continued to forgive him and trust him over and over and over again. It seemed that no matter what he did when he was drunk, you would start all over again as if nothing had happened. I felt so betrayed. These days I protect myself from you and keep you at a distance.

Whispered, rushed phone calls, raised voices, prolonged angry silences, outbursts of rage, lies and deceit are the norm in alcoholic homes. The sacred rituals that children should and might expect to enjoy in secure families are missing. Rituals such as meal-times together or story-time tucked up in bed at night are absent or at best intermittent. While active abuse of children in every form is clearly damaging, most of the difficulties are caused by neglect of ordinary parental duties. The absence of personal security, consistent love and affection and the presence of an emotionally volatile, unstable atmosphere create massive emotional problems for the children.

There are mountains of worries and issues to negotiate. Children may be dragged to the pub, spending hours in the car or in the car park or hanging around the bar area while their parent or parents are drinking. A woman told me that this occurred to her regularly over a three-year period when she was attending primary school, aged seven to ten, and in that time she was propositioned sexually by several drunks and groped by two strangers near the toilets. She was offered drink on numerous occasions by 'friends' of her father. She can distinctly remember the noxious stale smell of body odour, sweat, smoke and urine in that public house.

Then she would have to endure the journey home. She remembers desperately trying to keep her father awake as he drove down country lanes. She would watch him urinate by the side of the road or straight into his pants. Then, when they eventually arrived home after a traumatic day, she would try to get him to go to bed and clean him up. She would wait until he was comatose, remove the cigarette from his hand and then cover him with a blanket wherever he lay. Many times he would lie asleep across her bed and she would have to move to another room. Sometimes he would get the munchies and insist that she cook for him. If so, she would watch as he ate with his bare hands, and eventually relative peace would prevail.

Sometimes the torment for this child continued long into the night. He would wake up and shout for her to come to him with some drunken issue that was impossible to understand. At some stage in the small hours she would finally go to bed somewhere in the house and fall into an exhausted sleep. Then she would get up for school the next day, worn out and shattered, and of course fearful that schoolmates might find out the 'dirty' secret about her life at home. She had no one to confide in as her mother had died some years earlier.

Normalization

As noted in Chapter 3, there is a 'righting reflex' in all of us which tries to fix things. We try to make sense of situations and find a solution to them: it is a natural human response. In extreme circumstances this same righting reflex comes into play. Victims of abuse try to find some method to help them to deal in some way with issues that are incomprehensible and unacceptable. Thus, when growing up in a dysfunctional family unit, an attempt has to be made to normalize the events in some way in order to be able to survive.

Heather, now in her fifties, was brought up in a family where the father and mother were both alcoholics. There would be periods of quiet and moments of normality. I asked her if there had ever been violence and she answered, 'No,' but then went on to say that she was 'chastised' by her father when he was drunk. She actually said that the occasions were no more than anyone else would endure and also that the culture in those days was tolerant of corporal punishment.

In fact, it emerged that in her childhood, aged from about eight to 12, she was subject to the most awful beatings and humiliation that one would associate more with a concentration camp. The beatings were very severe, it transpired, and involved many forms of systematic torture. Her siblings were treated in the same way and they all witnessed one another's abuse. She was the only one who had sought help from counselling some 40 years later, and this was only because she found herself in another abusive alcoholic relationship as an adult.

The key point is that in some way in her own mind she had minimized the abuse and normalized it in order to cope. I guess we should not be surprised by this, as we know that people who are severely traumatized make up ingenious ways to survive. In Auschwitz, for example, some inmates managed to survive by living in the latrines.

Normalization has many forms and many results. For example, a young woman told me she was sexually abused, aged nine, by her uncle (her father's brother), a man in his forties at the time. She said she never wanted to do anything about it because he was a 'kind man' who gave her great help and support during her father's prolonged drinking periods.

Factors which might improve or exacerbate the situation for children

- The presence or absence of a non-drinking parent;
- prolonged exposure to abuse with few periods of hope or abstinence;
- the age of the child – but all children are damaged by alcohol abuse in the home;
- access to and bonds with other responsible adults in the community, family or wider circle of friends;
- availability and knowledge of help and support services;
- isolation – rural areas, for example;
- recovery, or lack of recovery, of the drinking parent and how quickly this occurs;
- support from siblings.

Specific conditions

Care should be taken with the following list of signs and symptoms that may indicate the existence of an alcohol problem in the homes of children. They may also indicate all sorts of other problems. Remember, all children are uniquely impacted when there is alcoholism in the home.

- Encopresis and enuresis (the technical terms for soiling and wetting incontinence);
- anxiety and social phobia;
- distress and sad appearance, tearful;
- depression (rare in younger children in its full clinical form);
- mood problems;
- acting up; trouble with the law or at school; bullying by peers, school phobia and other behavioural problems;
- developmental problems and slow learning;
- significant under-achieving or over-achieving at sport or in school;
- attention-seeking behaviour;
- stealing, telling lies;
- under-nourishment, under-development;
- fatigue, difficulty in concentration; looks tired, bags under the eyes;
- temper tantrums;
- old before his or her time;
- fretfulness;

- giddiness;
- nightmares;
- poor sleep pattern;
- eating disorders;
- attention deficit or hyperactivity;
- skin conditions and other childhood illnesses; more prone to infections;
- physical signs of abuse, such as bruising, burn marks, scratches, scrapes and bumps;
- unexplained incidents or accidents;
- poor hygiene;
- inappropriate sexual behaviour; exposing private parts or talking in a sexual manner inappropriate to the child's age;
- school refusal and absenteeism; paradoxically, children may be more clingy to the parent, believing that if they are present they may be able to stop the parent's problems.

Other issues for children

I will never forget hearing the following story from a female whose father was alcoholic when she was growing up. She had a pet that she adored, and one day, very drunk and in a fit of rage, he killed it with a shovel in front of her and her siblings in the back garden. She was deeply traumatized as a result of witnessing this piece of gross violence. This incident had understandably haunted her ever since and it never came to the attention of any authority.

Some colleagues of mine would say that the individual who did this must have had other issues, but I am not so sure about that. Cruelty to pets or getting rid of or damaging loved objects (toys, dolls, comfort blankets, etc.) is not uncommon in the homes of alcoholics. I think most behaviours are possible when someone is very drunk.

The children often hear or witness inappropriate behaviour from both parents. When drunk, parents may verbally assault their children and forget the whole conversation the next day. It is common, for example, to hear from teenage children that they have had inappropriate sexualized remarks made about their bodies when a parent is intoxicated. Children often hear parents arguing about sexual issues, or the drinking parent may 'confide' in his or her young child about the faults of the other parent in a way that is just wrong. One child, for example, aged six, was told by his father when very drunk that his mother was frigid and uninterested in sex.

Sometimes the absence of a reliable parent is acutely felt when things go wrong as a child. A young boy who was sexually abused by a stranger in a playground on his way home from school *could not* tell his parents what happened because his father was drinking heavily and would not care or understand, while his mother was too stressed. He told me he would only be adding to the mess that was his family, and therefore he chose to keep the abuse to himself.

Young children are often exposed to filthy situations. A young boy told me that he would have to clean up excrement on the walls and floors before going to bed when his father came home drunk.

Another young boy trained in martial arts to try to get ready to protect his mother from his violent drunken father.

Roles

In order to cope, children may adopt particular roles within the dysfunctional family. Family therapists have developed theories about such roles. There are many variations on this theme but usually they suggest that children fall into the following roles in families where alcohol problems occur:

Hero This child holds the family together and helps it to maintain a functioning appearance. He or she excels at school or sport. The family thinks that there cannot be too much wrong as this child is thriving. Inside, however, this child is hurting badly and craving recognition from the parents.

Lost child Sometimes called the 'withdrawn' or 'silent' child. This child tries to cause no problems in an attempt to make the troubles disappear. The parents think this child is quite happy, but in fact the child is in his or her own world and may be depressed.

Scapegoat Tends to act up and get into trouble. This child is typically blamed for all of the problems within the family. The child distracts the parents from other issues. The future for children in this role without help is to be always in trouble and to be looking for attention and affection.

Comic or mascot The role of this child is to reduce stress and tension through humour. Inside, this child is crying hard.

I have only briefly mentioned this systemic theory and have not done justice to the many layers and explanations for these roles and others. There have been volumes written about it. In reality, children often fall into and out of all these roles, as noted by family therapist and author Sharon Wegscheider Cruse, who has worked widely in this area. Such revelations have led to the formation of the National Association of Children of Alcoholics (NACOA) self-help groups, set up to support those harmed by living with alcoholism as children.

Frequently asked questions

I am desperate to get away from my most abusive wife. I have taken legal advice and though it won't be easy we can get a legal separation or a divorce, but I am worried that our young children will be damaged by the separation. Are children always damaged by marital breakdown?

I think the only honest answer here is yes, children are usually deeply upset by any marital separation. Are they damaged, though? Yes, certainly in the short term. In the lead-up to a separation and in the immediate aftermath there is inevitably emotional damage to the children.

Children struggle to understand the issues involved and have a sense of abandonment. They often have the upheaval of having to move home or of having two homes because of access and custody issues. This leads to all sorts of practical problems, such as seeing friends and where to keep their schoolbooks. They are sometimes torn apart because they feel compelled to make judgements of their parents or feel that they have to side with one or other parent. Therapists often see adults who are still traumatized by separation that occurred in their childhood. It is not so much the actual separation that distressed them, however, but the bitterness, rancour and disputes which preceded and followed it that caused most of the unhappiness.

Preparation for the split is most important to help the children avoid the worst aspects of this social reality. When relationships break down it is imperative, wherever possible, to try to behave like mature adults and not allow the children to see or hear the worst disagreements. Regrettably, this is seldom the case. Many children have told me that they did not know what was going on at the time of their parents' divorce or separation. Many were left wondering if they were the cause of their parents splitting. In addition, children often worry that one or other of the parents has some sort of terminal illness as there are so many unexplained tears and whispered calls and conversations before the separation.

It is often said that children are resilient, and while this is true great care should be taken to try to protect them at the time of the separation and long after the break-up has occurred. Finally, it has to be acknowledged that staying in an abusive relationship can be more damaging for children than separation.

Are my children at risk of developing alcoholism? I have heard that it is hereditary and both my wife and I are in recovery from alcoholism.

The jury is still out as regards the part genetics plays in alcoholism, and the question reveals a fear and anxiety that most people in recovery share. The truth is that genetics probably does play some part, but exactly how and why it hits some of the children in a family while others avoid it is not clear. Circumstances, individual aspects and life events are all also important in the development of alcohol problems. Hereditary factors and social factors probably combine with individual factors such as personality to 'create' alcohol problems in an individual.

Perhaps the closest we can come to the truth with our current knowledge is that hereditary aspects and environmental factors are both relevant. Alcoholism can skip generations, and perhaps this lends weight to the environmental factor. A typical sequence may be that the grandfather had an alcohol problem so his son is extra careful and does not drink at all, but then the grandson, in the third generation, develops alcohol dependence. This explanation is clearly over-simplistic, however.

The most protective thing that you can do as parents in recovery is to be as honest as possible about your problem with the children in an age-appropriate manner, and obviously to be the best parents you can be and to lead by example.

6

Why might they want me to drink?

'Go on, go on, go on': driven to drink

Mrs Doyle, in the hit Channel 4 comedy series *Father Ted*, famously 'makes' people drink tea by the exhortation, 'Go on, go on, go on, go on . . .' (ad nauseam). In the UK and Ireland, the norm in social situations is not for tea to be foisted on you but for alcohol to be 'pushed' on you, sometimes aggressively. In this context we are nations of Mr and Mrs Doyles!

'A bird never flew on one wing', 'Have one for the road', 'Just have one', 'Will you have one later?', 'Get that into you and relax' are examples of typical comments made when encouraging people to use alcohol.

There is scant or no regard for people who choose not to drink. People who do not want to drink may have very good reasons for choosing that option, or they may decide not to drink for no particular reason at all, but in fact in social situations they are often pressurized to drink alcohol. At parties, get-togethers, barbecues, weddings, funerals, sporting and other entertainments it is expected that people will drink alcohol, and indeed drink a lot. The social etiquette is for alcohol to be available for any occasion, and regular heavy drinking is now commonplace. To be a non-drinker in such a climate can be very challenging. It is easier to comply and hard to resist in such circumstances. Of course, one can say no, but this is not easy if you are down on your luck, anxious or lacking in social skills and confidence. Not easy either, for example, if you are just out of rehabilitation or if you have started to attend Alcoholics Anonymous.

There is huge subtle and overt pressure to be 'normal' and to conform. As evenings go on and people get more and more tipsy, and in many cases rude and offensive, non-drinkers in the party can become very isolated and made to feel extremely uncomfortable. With drinks on board and inhibitions loosened, they can be harangued or even confronted. 'Did you have a problem in the past?', 'Why are you such a dry stick?', 'Are you afraid to have fun?', 'Are you judging me?', 'Do you think you are better than me?' These are just some of the examples of remarks made to people in recovery that I hear regularly. It seems that any tiny hesitance or reluctance to conform is instantly sensed and inquisitions are thus innocently provoked.

This cultural problem is so extensive that people who are trying to abstain require coaching as to how to handle such situations. I often encourage people to have a script ready before they go out, especially in early recovery. For example, 'I used to drink but I don't now', 'Doctor's orders', 'I'm on a health kick', or 'I'm off it for Lent', or 'for a few months'. Some simply tell the truth: 'I have a problem with alcohol.' The key point, in order to escape further embarrassment or, worse, giving in to demands to drink, is to be firm and comfortable with whatever line is used.

There is little sympathy or understanding for people who stay in an abusive relationship, too. Casual social chats often reveal insensitivity to those trapped in unfortunate relationships. 'It would only have to happen once for me to leave if he did that', 'Why don't they call for help?', 'Why doesn't she just kick him out?' and so on.

Alcohol problems: a logical response to unhappy relationships?

Most people would expect partners to be supportive of each other in the case of an alcohol problem, at least in the short term. Like any other worrying situation in a relationship, a partner would be hopeful that the person with an alcohol problem would make a full recovery, and would make all reasonable attempts to help her. In the vast majority of situations this is indeed the case and partners are remarkably supportive, even in the long term. However, in a smaller number of cases the opposite occurs: sometimes people with drink problems are actively encouraged to drink by their partners.

There are numerous simple and complex reasons for such behaviour. In my work I have often seen family members urging their problem drinker to continue to drink, or creating situations where they are likely to revert to drinking. Some of this may be due to ignorance – they just do not understand that the person should not drink – or sometimes it is a response based on ill-judged pity and wanting the person to be 'normal'.

There are other more complex explanations, however. Alcohol, paradoxically, can square circles in the short term. In other words, alcohol can make impossible situations bearable. Individuals who find themselves in deeply unhappy relationships can use alcohol to help them to cope with that reality.

Two typical examples might illustrate this method of coping:

1 A woman may use alcohol to allow her to lower her inhibitions sufficiently to be able to have sex in an abusive or unsatisfactory relationship with her husband.
2 A man who is having multiple affairs may actively want his partner to be drunk so that she does not notice or discover his infidelity, or so that she does not care.

Drinking alcohol may represent, in part, a resistance to controlling within the relationship.

Virginia, a lady in her forties, is married to a man with a job which involves being in the public eye. She has had multiple previous treatments for alcoholism. She would drink in binge patterns, vast quantities, and get absolutely hammered to the point that she was almost totally unaware of her surroundings and would rarely remember the events of the evening. These binges always happened at the time that would cause maximum embarrassment to her husband during social events. She would be inappropriately dressed and foul-mouthed, and would scream to people, most of whom were strangers, about her unhappy life and marriage. When the public had retired home for the night he would beat her up for her bad behaviour, and she would then lie low, licking her wounds and full of embarrassment till the next drinking occurrence would come around, and so the pattern continued for many years until she finally gained sufficient insight and managed to abstain from alcohol.

In treatment, with careful prompting, she described a very controlling man to whom she was married, with a history of violence to her long before they ever got married. She believed that he wanted to be married to a subservient person, a person that she said she could not be. Yet in a strange and bizarre way her drinking somehow kept them together for years. It is as if she was saying, '**** you, I will show you that there are some areas that you cannot control.' We could call this the '****U syndrome', in short. It is rather rude and crude, but very common, and partly explains some complex dynamics that perpetuate addictive behaviours. Basically the partner is saying: '****U, you will not control this part of my life. I will drink if and when I want to.' Some people may dismiss it as an excuse for drinking, but I certainly believe it is an important factor. The partner, in classic instances of resentful retaliation, may respond with further molten anger until the spiral of trench warfare is so complicated it makes little sense at all to someone watching from the outside.

Barbara, a woman in her fifties, explained that shortly after one particular in-patient treatment she was dropping her husband off at the airport. When he got out of the car she noticed that he had left a full litre bottle of spirits on the back seat. She duly drank it. There followed further hospital admissions and life-threatening health consequences.

When her husband was questioned about this incident, he said that he had left it there 'as a test to see if she could resist'. This does not make sense. Even allowing for distress, anxiety and some desperation in coping with someone in the family who drinks, it does not fully explain such behaviour. In this particular case it was eventually discovered that he was having multiple affairs. Some might speculate that if his wife was drunk he would seek 'solace' elsewhere. The only conclusion I could come to was that it suited him for his wife to continue to drink. When drunk she was less likely to discover or confront his behaviour.

Fred, in his forties, had had three separate treatments for alcohol problems in the previous decade. Five years ago it came to a head again when he was admitted for physical complications associated with his alcohol problem. He talked of a deeply unhappy and disturbed relationship where his wife was verbally, emotionally and physically abusive. In marital sessions she admitted to violence that pre-dated his alcohol dependence. He bitterly complained that everything in treatment centres was put down to his drinking but that this was only a part of the story. He is now many years sober and he and his wife are still together, having done a lot of soul-searching and considerable marital work.

Some couples eventually split, of course, and then in certain cases the controlling behaviour of the non-drinking partner becomes more evident. I have been involved in hundreds of bitter separation cases where legal action has been sought, involving disputes over money, accommodation, child custody and access. The court would not be involved if the parties concerned were able to come to an amicable and mutually satisfying resolution, but some of the behaviour regarding the children from a bitter parent is incomprehensible. A significant number of such parents seem to be unconcerned about mutual care of the children, but rather are focused on who 'wins' and who gains the most. Bitterness is one aspect of this, but there are also instances of cruelty and punishment. For example, some people in recovery are not even allowed to see their own children – that is, they are not permitted to set eyes upon them – and are also refused any form of access to them. Hence, court action is necessary.

I have seen situations where partners have part-engineered in-patient treatment for their partners with the long-term goal of using that event to gain control of goods and the children. Many people are therefore on the back foot when the separation starts, even though they too might be living with a partner who has an alcohol or drug problem that is unrecorded and undiagnosed. Evidence is paramount in court.

One man said to a client of mine, in recovery from alcoholism, in reference to his own violence: 'The beauty of this, honey, is that you can prove nothing and you have been to a treatment centre – it is a matter of public record.'

In many cases children have to be protected by the court from parents who are in active addiction; what I am referring to here is the situation where the drinker is in recovery but bitterness and control-ling behaviour lives on in the ex-partner. I am talking here of excessive control issues rather than ones of practical necessity.

Unresolved issues

I once tried to describe partners of problem drinkers as having unre-solved personality issues, as follows: 'Suffering Susan', 'Controlling Catherine', 'Wavering Winifred' and 'Punitive Polly'. The theory was developed by a caseworker, Thelma Whalen, in the United States. Is it possible that certain personality traits are indeed attracted to living with alcoholism? Of course, it is a sexist theory and maybe if 'Sean', 'Charles', 'Wally' and 'Peter' were included, it would be a little more apt and have more universal appeal. Unresolved issues within the partner are very important.

A lady in her forties, who had had an alcohol problem but had not been drinking for over four years, wrote a piece in counselling about her relationships with men. She was trying to understand her past pat-terns of drinking, and trying to avoid repetition of past relationship patterns in future ones. She wondered why she was constantly attracted to emotionally unavailable men. She also described how she would go into a tail spin if she experienced an insinuated or actual put-down, and 'ruthlessly internalize this negativity and start to drink again'. In her specific case there was a history of sexual abuse by her father, and this may explain the triggering of negative self-esteem at the hands of a man. Tellingly, she wrote:

> I have to try too hard to get affection from a man. I consider his sexual needs over mine. I feel that sex is the only confirmation that he cares

for me. I have punished myself over and over again by drink and other self-destructive patterns for men's bad treatment of me.

This is perhaps an obvious example of drink in a weird way squaring circles and making incompatible relationships tolerable. There are many other more subtle forms for such transactions.

Many people feel justified in the way they treat a partner because that partner is an alcoholic. It is as if the normal rules do not apply because she is drinking. Anything goes. A man told me that he had physically attacked his wife because he was at the end of his tether. She was left so badly beaten that she required medical help, and the bruising and marks were so severe that she could not leave her home for five days. While one can understand how frustrating it is to live with someone who will not or cannot change, physical violence can never be justified. Apart from moral objections to such issues, it is also completely ineffective if the goal was to try to stop the person from drinking. There are other choices and ways of managing: he could walk away or leave.

Enmeshment

Sir Walter Scott's famous lines, 'Oh what a tangled web we weave/ When first we practise to deceive' are never more relevant that in intimate relationships that are dominated by alcohol. After years of all sorts of '****U syndrome' complications, grief, hurt, anger, resentment, attempts to manipulate and control, on both sides of the divide, it sometimes becomes almost hopelessly entwined and very hard to unravel. In many cases the situation eventually burns out and the couple stay together with little vision or sound. Many couples separate not because of the drinking but because of some other jarring piece of new reality, such as desperate financial circumstances or proven infidelity.

If the couple are to have any hope of sorting things out together, in my view, the very first step must be abstinence, and there follows a lengthy process of counselling. For this to succeed, both parties need to lay down their weapons, especially the verbal ones, and to have a fresh, honest look at their own behaviour. The two people must be willing to engage openly and fully in working together to resolve their own mess. This is fraught with difficulty and resembles a tightrope act. In therapy, even within ten minutes of explaining everything carefully and asking the couple to listen afresh to each other, focusing not on the areas the other needs to change but rather on what they themselves can do to improve things, the situation can break down into a haranguing session. If that happens with a stranger present, what are things like at home? Yet remarkably many people stick with the process and achieve disentanglement and get on with their lives.

Sometimes one partner is just too hurt or exhausted after numerous relapses, and the other is so full of resentment that he does not realize that he is actually constantly angry with her. She can now do nothing right, even if she stays sober. If this is the case the couple may be doomed to a life of resentment and rancour if they are unable to separate or sort out these dynamics.

Sometimes a sad aspect of recovery is when the person with the alcohol problem moves on but leaves her long-suffering partner behind. An individual goes into treatment and gets help and insight. Meanwhile her partner is outside, taking care of the home and the children. He is not therefore able to avail himself of the same level of help. Sometimes the person in treatment starts to feel really good about herself and becomes attracted to other people who are also emerging out of their own negative cocoon. Although not common, relationships can occur in such settings, and the partner at home is further traumatized and distraught.

Another potential banana skin on the road to recovery for couples is a difficulty in letting go of fear and anxiety. He is often ambiguous about his partner's recovery for fear that it will all fall apart. He is thinking, 'I'll hold something back in terms of trust or belief in case my world will fall apart again.' This is sensed by his partner, and the spiral of destruction may be set in motion again.

It is also not uncommon in partners' groups to hear people saying that they were more sick than their partner who had the alcohol problem.

One man summed it up like this:

Yes, of course she had a drink problem, but on reflection my behaviour was much worse that hers before I went for help. I became totally obsessed and my only goal in life was to try to stop her from drinking. I was like a private eye or a detective following her round and trying to catch her out. I suffered dreadfully and neglected myself completely. I had high blood pressure, headaches and was full of anxiety and fear. Needless to say, I could not stop her from drinking and this only served to make me more obsessive and controlling. In therapy, I stepped back from it all and could see what I was doing, and I discovered that there were deeper issues in our relationship than the drinking behaviour of her good self.

Another partner in counselling:

> I was totally involved in trying to stop him from drinking. I got very sick as a result and required treatment for depression. The only thing that I could compare it to is trying to come to terms with my father's death. I used to think I saw him when I was walking down a street after he died, and I knew this was a normal part of bereavement, but one day during the worst of my husband's drinking I was sure, on my way home from work, that I saw his car outside a pub; it turned out to be a similar car so it was my own fear and anxiety gone mad. Even though I knew he wasn't in the pub I proceeded to have a massive row with him, as though he had in fact been there.

Needless to say, such controlling behaviour, though understandable, puts extra pressure on the relationship.

Enmeshment requires disentanglement, but sometimes the knots are too hard to unravel. There is a situation in chess called *Zugzwang*. The term does not translate from the German simply, but roughly, in chess, it means that the system is completely blocked and the player who is about to move has to lose something. The move will relieve the system but it does not necessarily mean that the game is lost. In alcoholic families the same type of situation often applies. If the situation is to be relieved or disentangled, one or both players have to make a move that will lead to some loss, but might entail a solution further on. For example, one party may have to stop drinking while the other one may have to lose resentment.

Deeper issues

People 'find' themselves in relationships with people who have complicated personal issues. This was also touched on in Chapter 3.

One alcoholic lady who had a number of children with her husband discovered that he was homosexual, and could not cope with this reality. In some rare cases partners cross-dress, while some have transgender issues. Some have sexual preferences that their partners do not approve of. Some people have told me that their problem drinking began when they discovered that their partners were into pornography. Such issues are important factors in the development of alcohol problems and add to the complexity of relationships.

In my early career I met a couple who both had serious alcohol problems and both accepted treatment. As far as I know, to this day they are both sober and in new healthy relationships. They both agreed that they met when drunk, got engaged when drunk, married when drunk and separated when drunk – in short, they were drunk for the five years when they were together before they split. They were refreshingly honest!

In many cases it is more complicated, but some people have strong reasons why they may want their partner's drinking to continue.

Frequently asked questions

If I understand you right, it sounds as if you are blaming the partner for the alcoholic's drinking.

The point I want to make is that alcohol problems are rarely simple or linear but rather are complicated and multifaceted. There are many deep layers to alcohol problems. These layers become further complicated or enmeshed over time and they require careful, sensitive disentanglement. The therapy or approach to helping should never be about blame, but rather one of understanding and resolution. Some behaviours of an alcoholic can never be excused. However, there are certain situations that defy ordinary logic, and undoubtedly the controlling behaviour of some partners and other personal factors need to be understood and unravelled if the overall situation is to be helped.

My wife went into residential treatment and came out sober but with a new relationship. Our marriage ended shortly afterwards, and I feel so bitter.

This is a question I have been asked a number of times.

Unfortunately, this does happen, though the specific circumstances you mention are rare. Infidelity is a fact of life and occurs even when no alcohol problem exists. The hurt is obviously enormous in every case. There is a special sense of betrayal in this particular instance, perhaps, after you have invested so much in your wife's recovery. I would recommend that you spend some time with a therapist and explore the circumstances and all of the various feelings involved, so that you can try to get over the hurt and resentment. Such emotions will only serve to infect your own life.

7

Types of available help

This chapter and the next two are all about helping services and practical and emotional help.

Asking for help is usually a scary step, with all sorts of associated fears and anxieties. The individual partner is concerned that she might be judged or even ridiculed, and another major problem is a sense of disloyalty. Even if your partner knows that you have decided to see someone to get help, it seems as if you are going behind his back when you go looking for advice and support.

So in this chapter I want to try to address some of these issues and answer some questions in the hope that people will be reassured as to what actually goes on in counselling. Hopefully some myths will be debunked, and with all this new information people might be more likely to access the various forms of help that are available.

What to expect from professional help

Going for help equates to admitting that your own efforts to sort out the relationship have failed. This in itself is an obstacle to help-seeking. It is probably difficult for people who do not have major problems in their relationships to understand this basic fact. It is not easy to expose your most intimate emotional areas to the scrutiny of a stranger, even though that stranger is a professional. If you reveal your innermost thoughts and feelings you are automatically more vulnerable and perhaps even suspicious of questioning.

People sitting opposite a counsellor, psychologist, nurse or doctor may have all sorts of thoughts in their heads and emotions in their hearts. Does he like me? Is she disgusted with me? Will he believe me? Will she laugh at me? Does he think I am stupid? Are my troubles trivial compared to what she normally hears? Will he take my partner's side because they are the same gender? Should I tell her that? Will he be offended if I use bad language?

They may also believe the whole thing to be a waste of time. These questions and doubts are present long before the person actually takes the seat opposite a therapist. Consequently, people often attend for counselling long after the problem has begun, and as a result the problem is much harder to resolve as it is more established and entrenched. As a professional counsellor I would like to take the opportunity to reassure readers that the counsellor is *only* focused on the ways he or she might be of assistance to this particular person who has come looking for help.

People often have a particular issue or maybe many big issues in their heads that they are scared they might be made to disclose in counselling. Such 'biggies' could be defined as a major incident or event that the person finds extremely uncomfortable to talk about as it invokes horribly intense feelings of regret or shame. An obvious example would be marital rape, but there are all sorts of other personal issues. Everyone has their own particular 'biggie'. Such issues do not have to be disclosed early on in the counselling relationship, and never if so desired. However, the more you can get out in the open over time, the more likely it is that you can find a solution to your problems.

Counselling can also evoke memories that are very painful but may have been buried. These may well be affecting a person at some level, and in some cases may represent a major stumbling block to recovery.

Language can also be a major obstacle in counselling. Some partners of alcoholics may not have very good use of the local language or have great difficulty articulating their innermost turmoil, while some counsellors may not explain words or phrases carefully enough or may use unfamiliar jargon, leading to possible misinterpretations on both sides. Most counsellors will tell people to ask if something is unclear and should know when something is not properly understood. The counsellor should ask questions such as 'Do you understand what I mean by that?' or 'How do you feel about that?' If something is said that, on reflection, you do not like or understand, you should ask for clarification at the next session.

I remember years ago talking to a male alcoholic in treatment and I suggested that he was 'thick', by which I meant he was stubborn or resistant to change. It was certainly a very bad choice of words anyway, made worse by the fact that where he came from, 'thick' meant 'stupid'.

Recently, in discussion with a man about sexual issues, he explained that his wife had been very manipulative and bullying in that area of their lives together in his younger years. He was extremely distressed about this as it was still affecting their current level of intimacy. It was a long conversation, and I reassured him as best as I could that this was an important issue. Perhaps too casually, I said that he would need to accept what happened and try to move on. Once again this was misunderstood to mean that he should accept what happened in the sense that it was justified. Luckily this was clarified within the session.

What should you look out for?

In writing this chapter I am trying to assure people that good counselling is available. However, it assumes that we are talking about professional people who are bound, by the ethics of their own association or professional body, to behave properly and appropriately. If you are not satisfied with any aspect of counselling you have the right to complain, and such a complaint should be taken very seriously by the counsellor concerned. It will certainly be considered very carefully and processed if it is formalized and sent in writing to the relevant professional body. There are all sorts of rules of engagement and boundaries that the counsellor must adhere to.

The basics that you are entitled to, and which would be universal 'rules' for most professional accrediting bodies, are as follows:

- You should be seen in a private area where your conversation is not overheard.
- You should be treated with respect, common courtesy, a non-judgemental approach and controlled emotional involvement. You should not be shouted at or ridiculed. You should be listened to intently.
- You should be allowed to request to see any notes that are taken.
- You should be entitled to confidentiality and have any limits to that confidentiality properly explained.
- You should ask questions about the terms and conditions and enquire about the counsellor's particular approach, experience and qualifications.
- You should know that you can walk out if you are not happy.
- You should discontinue sessions if you are not happy in any way.
- You should receive a receipt if it is a private consultation.
- You should have appropriate washroom facilities.

Many counsellors have such information on a fact sheet. Unfortunately, in some geographical areas counselling may be hard to access. Remember that you must first break the silence and ask for help. Take your courage in your hands and speak to your GP, perhaps, as a starting point. There is rarely a quick fix, though. Getting proper help is a process rather than a one-off event. The situation may not be capable of being fixed, as you might initially hope or expect (he stops drinking, happily stops, makes amends, works on the relationship with you and you all live happily together ever after). Other outcomes might come to pass, and this sometimes involves separation of some form.

Pick a counsellor as wisely as you can. Look for recommendations. I have to admit to a slight bias and preference for counsellors who have a professional background, such as in nursing, medicine, psychology or social work, as they are usually grounded in ethics and undergo more training. However, there are numerous outstanding counsellors who are the exceptions, and many people in recovery from alcohol problems themselves make excellent therapists. They must also have sufficient training and belong to some accrediting body.

You should always check whether the counsellor is accredited to some reputable professional organization. All such organizations ensure that their members adhere to strict codes of conduct, and it is important to remind you that they also all have 'fitness to practise' committees which investigate complaints. Enquire about the therapist's training background and professional qualifications. How much experience does this person have, and in what areas? Also ask if he or she has professional insurance.

If it is a group practice or agency, ask whether you will see the same person each time. On his first appointment in a particular institution, one man met a consultant psychiatrist who was extremely good and very helpful; however, in eight subsequent visits he never saw that individual again but instead saw stand-ins with fewer qualifications who were inadequately briefed on his case. Consequently he felt he received insufficient help, and clearly there was no proper continuity of care.

Sometimes the therapist will recommend more specialist forms of help, and if so should be able to provide you with recommendations. Examples here would be for marital therapy or sexual counselling.

Do not be put off by any past negative experiences. There are very experienced, caring professionals around, although sometimes it takes a while to find the right chemistry and you may need to try more than one before you get the right person to help you move on.

Getting the best out of counselling

You need to 'unglue' yourself! You need to become 'unstuck' from the situation and appreciate that you are embarking on a type of journey. Try to figure out what might be the destination. The end point is often unclear, however, as you start off. As with real journeys, you may stop off for a rest or many rests, or you may go in all sorts of different directions. The key aspect is to acknowledge that the journey is necessary and that you do need to take some steps to improve your situation. A therapist or doctor or nurse or some other person may be your guide on this journey, offering you support and encouragement and pointing out pitfalls along the way.

I often say to people that climbing a mountain looks very easy from a distance. It is only when you are up close that you realize that you are unable to see the top or that there are many barriers and valleys along the way. Prepare for the journey as best you can, decide who your guide(s) and support(s) might be and, when you are ready, set off.

In therapy you will usually be asked to talk about yourself and your own coping mechanisms, rather than about your partner or his drinking.

A tricky dilemma for a professional therapist is whether or not to see someone's partner having first counselled the person him or herself. Often one partner will be keen that 'her' therapist will see the other, especially if she is happy with the service she has received. However, it is usually better to suggest someone else for him, as it may become complicated as time goes on. It is a judgement call and depends on each individual case.

Self-help groups

Al-Anon

There are, thankfully, a number of self-help groups that can offer great support. Even to discover that there are many people who are coping and struggling with the same issues is a great help. There is a certain relief in knowing that you are not alone. When you look around a room full of people at a self-help group, you will notice both genders, all shapes and sizes and all creeds, religions and denominations.

Al-Anon is a self-help group for partners that has helped millions of people around the world. There are numerous groups in most localities and a proliferation in urban areas. Find out where your local meeting is. Just walk in and sit down and listen. You do not have to say anything if you do not want to. Typically, they will have a speaker at a meeting who is (or was) in the same boat as you, and then there are questions and answers. They are not dissimilar to Alcoholics Anonymous and also work on the basis of anonymity. If you are interested in attending a meeting, consult the Useful addresses section for contact details. If at all possible you should shop around until you find a meeting that you are comfortable at – they do vary. Attendance at Al-Anon and all the self-help groups listed is free, apart perhaps from a small donation to help pay for refreshments and literature.

Do not expect instant change. You need to go to meetings for your own sake. If you go to help your alcoholic partner and that is your only motivation, you are perhaps unlikely to succeed in the long run. It works best if you go to learn about yourself and your coping methods. Try and commit yourself to attending quite a number of meetings before you decide whether it suits you or not. In other words, stick at it to gain benefit.

Alateen

Alateen is available for the teenage children of alcoholics. Like all self-help groups, it works by establishing that you are not alone in coping with this issue and that other people with similar problems are willing to offer help and support. Many teenagers have said that they received great comfort and support from meeting other children living with alcohol problems.

National Association of Children of Alcoholics (NACOA)

NACOA self-help groups are not as widely available as Al-Anon but have a strong network and many meetings in the UK and Ireland. As already discussed in Chapter 5, they offer support to people who have experienced harm as a result of being raised in an alcoholic home.

Others

There are all sorts of other community and local support groups that can be of great assistance to partners of problem drinkers. They are not necessarily focused on alcohol or other addictions but offer advice and support to people who are struggling with personal issues. Many of them are listed in the Useful addresses section, but there are many more. Your GP, religious advisor or local community centre should be able to point you in the right direction. A partner may benefit, for example, from money and budgeting advice, or perhaps an assertiveness course or a parent and baby group. Many of these community-led initiatives are designed to give you practical support but also to help you to develop more confidence. If you are suffering from mental health issues there are other specific self-help groups available. Aware in Ireland and the Depression Alliance in the United Kingdom are well established and are of enormous help to people who are depressed and their families.

When attending any self-help group you should try not to compare your situation to that of others, but rather try to identify with feelings, thoughts and actions that other participants share. Take your time to suss out the participants; someone there may be a great help. Friendships are formed, and some of the self-help groups offer a type of 'buddy' or 'sponsor' system. This is usually where you are linked up with someone who is experienced and dependable and who you can ring or talk to in person to get support, especially in a time of crisis.

Groups may offer practical advice as well as emotional support.

Treatment centres

Partners often pin all their hopes on their loved one going for formal treatment, provided on an in-patient or out-patient basis. Out-patient facilities are more common and do vary, though they all tend to offer one-to-one and group therapy and some form of family support. Group therapy can be very helpful if you trust the process. It needs to be sensitively led, however.

Most residential treatment centres are private. They typically offer treatment for between two and five weeks, and are usually very expensive. Unless your partner has health insurance or an employer who is willing to subsidize treatment, he will have to pay, sometimes in advance before treatment commences. In some cases residential centres can take a number of patients free because they are subsidized by the state. Many centres assess the potential patient and the next of kin prior to admission. Depending on mental health issues, level of insight, length of sobriety, other drug use and much more besides, your partner may or may not be accepted. Sometimes the admission will be postponed until he has made some changes to his life. In some cases he will have to be sober for a period of time before he can be admitted.

Some treatment centres are in psychiatric settings, some in purpose-built units and some in old converted houses. Increasingly, the mental health services are offering treatment to people with dual disorders. The ethos and rules of the different residential treatment centres are also very varied and complicated, ranging from centres which allow residents to do practically whatever they want to places where there are rules for almost everything. Residents may not be allowed books, mobile phones or leave, for example.

Most treatment centres offer after-care, for which again there may be fees, and sometimes these extra costs have to be paid beforehand. The length of time and services provided during after-care vary greatly in different treatment centres. Typically, after-care runs for between one and two years. It consists of group therapy and sometimes one-to-one support. Family members are usually encouraged to attend as well.

I could make many more comments on all of the above, having worked in two very different residential settings. Suffice it to say that I empathize with anyone trying to get a partner into treatment, because there is such confusion and so many myths around the various different approaches. It would be great if there was an independent body or central assessment agency that could provide accurate information on available help for people with alcohol problems and their families.

Partners should research treatment facilities very carefully and again consult with health advisors and counsellors to avoid having unrealistic expectations. Millions of people are in recovery because of the help they have received from every type of facility, but it will not work for everyone. Check out too what services, if any, are offered specifically for the partner and also for the children. Family days are almost universal, but courses for partners and information for children are also provided by some centres. Finally, if a couple are going for assessment at any treatment centres I tell them that they too should make their own assessment of the treatment centre and think carefully before they decide to proceed.

Primary care

The most accessible source of help for people with alcohol problems and their partners is in primary care. The only problem here is that general practice is so terribly busy that the GP and practice nurses have little time to screen for alcohol problems or indeed to get very involved in the specific process of change. Governments have begun to realize that resources need to be pumped into this area and that brief intervention training for primary care personnel is both relatively cheap and effective. Brief interventions can be easily taught and involve the GP or practice nurse doing a quick alcohol assessment on the person, evaluating his or her readiness to change and providing information, in leaflet form for example, on alcohol. Success rates for such an approach – usually based on the range of problem drinking that presents in primary care and reductions in consumption – are very good throughout the world. It is true to say that brief interventions are more effective for hazardous and harmful drinkers. Thus primary care can provide most of the needs of the patient and his family discreetly on his doorstep.

Counsellors are part of the team in some primary care facilities, but regrettably the integration of counselling services and the use of brief interventions are not well developed in primary care in many geographical areas. We conducted two studies in the Irish College of General Practitioners in conjunction with the Health Service Executive (the Irish equivalent of the NHS) that proved the efficacy of counselling and brief interventions for alcohol problems in primary care. These two studies involved, in total, over 5,000 patients. The results were very encouraging in that 30 per cent of patients got significant help from a relatively inexpensive initiative. Many partners, too, were able to gain help that they may not otherwise have received.

General hospitals

Some general hospitals, no doubt alarmed about the number of problem drinkers and family members in their wards and out-patient services, have commenced brief interventions too. This is a very welcome development. Many patients attending Accident and Emergency departments have significant alcohol problems but rarely receive any form of advice or counselling owing to the mayhem in crisis medicine departments. Partners can look to the social work services, which are well established in general hospitals, for help and support, or in some cases the assistance of a specialist nurse or counsellor for alcohol problems.

Unless you are in an extremely remote geographical area there are a number of alternative local sources of help. (If you are in a very remote area, travel to get help!) Sometimes there is a need to access many different services. For example, a partner may attend a professional counsellor as well as the GP and a psychiatrist, and also attend Al-Anon.

In my experience, partners can get help from sources that perhaps you might not expect. For example, one partner was advised by a police officer where to get help after a domestic dispute, and the couple never looked back. In another case, a solicitor referred a partner for counselling. Spiritual leaders, employee assistance programmes, occupational health doctors, specialist physicians and surgeons have also been instrumental in starting people on the process of change. One man told me that he confided in his barber about his wife's drinking; the barber gave him the name of a specialist counsellor and his wife made a full recovery.

The next two chapters look at the nuts and bolts of the change process in more detail.

Frequently asked questions

Can therapy make things worse? I went to a counsellor about my husband's drinking and the situation definitely got worse.

This is an age-old question and is hard to answer in simple terms. The short answer is that therapy itself should never make things worse. Of course, if someone looking for help was unfortunate enough to meet a counsellor who was behaving in an unethical or unprofessional manner (e.g. siding with one or other party) things could go from bad to worse. Thankfully, this scenario is extremely rare. People need to appreciate that counselling puts a focus on the nature and extent of the problems within the relationship and therefore inevitably brings matters to a head. This can be very upsetting and sometimes overwhelming. The time you choose to get help is all-important. Is the individual or the couple ready to engage in counselling and reveal their innermost issues? For most people, however, talk therapy provides pain relief and things tend to improve slowly once the issues are addressed properly.

Another point for people considering couples therapy is that 'it takes two to tango' and if one partner is unwilling to get involved there is very little that can be done by the therapist. Sometimes one party in the relationship arrives in the therapy room with less than full commitment to change things round. An individual can therefore sabotage attempts to help because he or she is happy with things as they are. In some cases the couple need to consult a solicitor, not a counsellor.

In couples work where alcohol problems are significant, people should again be made aware of the notion of short- and long-term gain. Problem drinking gives short-term relief from issues and pain but long-term suffering, whereas, in recovery, therapy should be the other way round: short-term pain and long-term relief.

Should everything be discussed in counselling? I attended a counsellor who encouraged my wife and me to be completely honest with each other and to share all aspects of my drinking. I revealed that I had been seeing another woman, and when this was opened up we found that there was too much hurt and anger and we broke up.

This is a question I have been asked a number of times.

Obviously each couple need to decide how much information should be shared about personal or traumatic events in their lifetime together. Honesty is important in a relationship, but in relationships that have been dominated by alcohol, honesty and trust are two major casualties. Great care should be taken about disclosure of hidden incidents. Their revelation can cause more problems than they cure in most cases. Couples need to be careful about 'reckless honesty', as discussed in Chapter 2.

Most couples are acutely aware of this balancing act and know that to reveal hidden events may only be wise if the other partner is at risk, for example, from a sexually transmitted disease. Experienced counsellors will guide couples through this emotional minefield.

Sometimes a couple will be invited for a session where a partner will explain in detail about her painful experiences and feelings living with the alcohol problem. This can be very beneficial if it is carefully explained, if both parties agree and if it is made clear that this is only one aspect of the relationship that is going to be discussed.

Absolute truth sessions about all aspects of the relationship are usually detrimental to couples. Remember that although couples are seen together they are usually invited for one-to-one sessions where such tricky issues can be discussed individually.

8

What can I do? Psychological and emotional help

This chapter is about making changes to your life and how you might approach this difficult issue if you are living with a problem drinker. Chapter 9 deals with more practical aspects of change. This chapter is about psychological and emotional change.

I have always been fascinated and intrigued by the process of change and how some people manage to achieve and maintain positive change and, of course, why some people do not. The timing of personal change remains of great interest to me. Why do people come for help at this particular moment? This is not just a matter of academic curiosity – if we could find out more about such matters, we could develop services and treatment facilities accordingly, helping people more effectively and using money and resources more appropriately to develop the necessary tools and skills for practitioners.

Although much has been written about these matters, we are still unsure as to why people set off on their journey of change and exactly how they manage to achieve positive outcomes.

Is it something said by a friend, family member or stranger that initiated the change? Is it that the person is sick of being sick, in the sense that she has reached her own 'personal rock bottom' and therefore the only way, then, is up? Is it because the individual reaches a certain age or stage in life? Is it because of something the GP or some other health professional has mentioned in passing? Has one of these health professionals advised change during a brief intervention, for example? Is quick advice, given respectfully, as effective as counselling sessions or years attending self-help groups, or should they all be used in combination? Is it because of something people have heard or seen in the print media or on TV? Do people change in spite of or because of professional help? Does interviewing style matter to help create change? Why do some people 'relapse' into old habits, either quickly or after many years of positive changes, while others who make the changes never look back? Do people make lifestyle changes because of the persistence of their partner or some other family member? Do people get a flash of insight from some incident, like something a child might say when Dad is drunk, for example?

The answer to all of the above is yes, but what works is different in every case. To use another analogy, 'different locks are opened by different keys'.

As we grow older, change of any type is very difficult to achieve. Even small changes are hard to accomplish as we are creatures of habit and routine. It is true too that even positive change is not easy to incorporate into our daily lives. Nevertheless, every day, people find the strength within themselves to begin the process of change. The difficulty is to maintain that change and not fall back. I understand that after Christmas, for example, fitness centres and gyms can offer new membership to a multiple of those that they can actually accommodate because they know that a high percentage of people will drop out of their memberships once the resolutions start to wane.

It is now many years since two American researchers, James Prochaska and Carlo DiClemente, offered the 'wheel of change' as a template. The diagram in Figure 4 continues to be used in training of healthcare professionals throughout the world because of its simplicity. It depicts movement though several stages of change and is very useful in consultation with someone who is willing to contemplate change of any kind.

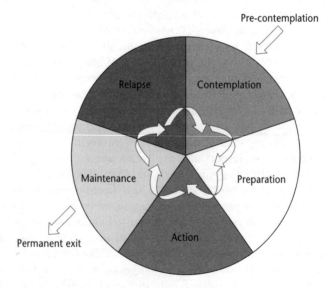

Figure 4 The wheel of change (original)

Though it has been criticized, like every other model of change, it still remains a good pictorial depiction of what change is all about, and how we might come to consider it and then carry it out. Of course, people do not fit into such neat categories in real life and may find themselves in several segments of the wheel at one and the same time. The time frame for such changes is not clear either. People may go through the wheel at a rapid rate or it may take years. I showed this to a young alcoholic some years ago and he told me that he was in 'contemplation', (thinking about change) when inside the clinic but that he was in 'relapse' as soon as he was in the car park!

The main advantage of the model is that it embodies the idea of changing position and doing something different to effect change. People with alcohol problems are initially 'pre-contemplators', in that they have no intention of changing their behaviour because they see no need to do so. Lapses and 'relapses' are common in this model of change and might, sometimes, even be a necessary part of lasting change.

The wheel is relevant to the partner too. The pre-contemplating partner of the alcoholic may have no idea of the need for change, and then some event or experience may catapult him into 'contemplation'. Relapse for the partner might mean falling back into his old ways

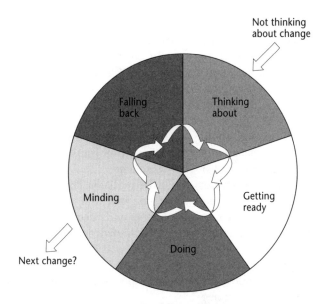

Figure 5 The wheel of change in plain English

by covering up for his alcoholic partner or making excuses for her behaviour.

I prefer the wheel in plain English, however (see Figure 5 on page 83). People relate much more easily to this diagram as the stages are easier to understand.

The big task for partners in all this is to somehow free themselves from the painful emotions that stop them from getting that wheel moving, such as guilt, shame, anger, fear, past issues, depression and other mental health issues. Trusting a professional therapist who can walk you through these phases at your own pace is an important way of starting the change process. So too are self-help groups, as discussed in Chapter 7. Exploring and expressing your innermost feelings is what is necessary.

The Serenity Prayer (see the Appendix), used so powerfully and effectively in Alcoholics Anonymous meetings, is actually relevant for everyone and especially for partners of problem drinkers. The decision about what you can change and what you cannot, as well as discerning and accepting the difference, is what that prayer is all about. Making changes to your life is a long process, but there are many simple steps that you might consider if you are living with alcohol problems.

Simple steps

- Make some small adjustment that makes your life a little better. The individual who is 30 years sober always has to start with today, so even a tiny movement in the right direction may be highly significant. An example might be to decide that you will not engage in the same old argument when your partner comes home drunk. The metaphor is withdrawing fuel from the flame.
- Ask someone for help. There must be someone out there who will be helpful and understanding. Asking for help serves several purposes: it makes you realize and establish within yourself that you need help, and it stops you from being isolated.
- Tell someone you can trust about the problem. This is a little deeper than the previous suggestion. If you can find someone that you trust, then you can delve a little further and open up about the worst aspects of your situation, safe in the knowledge that it will not be the subject of gossip or ridicule.
- Ring a support group or helpline. There are many different agencies that offer phone line support or personal counselling. (See the Useful addresses section.)
- Treat yourself – to a day off, or a half-day, or even a few hours away

from the hassle, or to some form of help or counselling. The key here is the word 'treat'. I always advise partners to focus on small and large treats as part of the solution to feeling better, but it has to be continuously worked at. People need to be reminded that they have the right to treat themselves. Go for a massage or for some exercise. Sit somewhere quietly.

- Make sure you do not believe that you deserve this treatment. Recently a partner said to me that she was injured by her husband *because* she answered him back. In using such language, she revealed that she believed that it was her fault and nothing to do with the fact that he was drunk!
- Use affirmations. For example, 'I deserve better', 'I do not deserve this treatment' and 'I am a good person.' They may sound trite but they work if they are repeated and developed.
- Recognize unacceptable behaviour for what it is, *unacceptable*.
- Read literature on the subject.
- Examine your own personal barriers to recovery. List the pros and cons of change and the pros and cons of no change.
- Process your own issues that pre-date the addictive behaviour. This usually requires professional assistance.
- Deal with the hurt and pain by talking about it and maybe writing about it.
- Remember to breathe properly. This is so important and often neglected. People who are stressed forget to breathe properly. They take breaths that are too shallow or short, and this serves to add to stress as not enough oxygen is moving through the lungs. Any doctor or therapist can explain this to you in more detail. It makes sense from an emotional perspective. If you are enjoying the view, you take your time and breathe in the scene. On the other hand, if what you see in front of you is very frightening, then you revert to survival mode and breathe in short bursts because you do not have time to breathe deeply.

The above ideas are in no particular order. Start somewhere. They may seem simple but can be very difficult if you have been neglecting yourself and not operating self-care. The overall message from these simple steps is that you should try to remember that you are a person in your own right, with your own needs and wants. This is not a dress rehearsal: this is your life.

A therapist may be necessary to help you with more traumatic or deeper personal issues and to perhaps guide you with any writing. If you do agree to write for therapy, remember that it is only for therapy and keep it carefully in a safe place. In therapy you may be asked challenging questions such as: 'Where do you see yourself in the next six months . . . the next year . . . five years . . .?' Such questions are designed to get movement going and to help you to envisage change at some stage in your life. You might also be asked to sketch a family tree, which may help you to see family patterns of behaviour over a longer period of time.

Partners and people with alcohol problems often ask if the process of talk therapy can be accurately described. Clearly it is about the relief gained from opening up, and the positive affirmation of being listened to carefully and respectfully. It is also about ongoing support and making plans, as well as the process of disentangling the story as discussed in Chapter 6. From my perspective, you could say that I see the person in front of me as a jigsaw puzzle. In most cases all of the pieces are there but some are stuck in the wrong places. My job is to help them to create the picture they want by putting the pieces of the jigsaw in the right position.

Relationship and family therapy

Instead of starting with the alcohol problem, many couples begin with some form of marital or couples therapy. If one of the couple is alcohol-dependent and does not stop drinking, this attempt is doomed to failure. Most therapists will quickly suggest that the problem drinker gets help for the drinking first. Once the drinking has stopped, the couple can explore their relationship in a relatively safe environment, usually in a series of sessions.

Some couples will need mediation services. These are only for couples who have decided to separate, and were introduced to reduce the legal costs of separation. They tend to be much quicker than the legal process, also reducing court costs. The couple go for a number of sessions where the issues are discussed, concluding with a written agreement which is rubber-stamped by the appropriate legal representatives.

Family therapy should only be conducted by trained family therapists. It examines internal family dynamics and offers suggestions as to how families might communicate and behave in a more effective and respectful way. Again, this is more effective if the drinking problems are resolved. Alcohol counsellors and other therapists routinely invite family members in for a family session, which needs to be handled very carefully if people are not to be traumatized further.

I often worry about the long-term consequences of one-off family sessions, where family members go home after the session and are unsure as to how the feedback has been assimilated by their loved one. Some people still hold to the naive view that the only object of such family sessions is to ensure that the person with the alcohol problem is clear about the damage she has done, and therefore will want to change. This is of course important, but there are many other dynamics at play. I run family sessions from time to time, but I prefer, if it is possible, to wait until the problem drinker is well on the road to recovery and able to understand the whole process. Furthermore, she should want to hear what her family has to say in the knowledge and belief that it is meant to be helpful and healing, and might possibly prevent relapse.

Tips for parents to help children cope

- Use helplines (see the Useful addresses section).
- Realize that children from a family where there is an alcohol problem have a statistically higher chance of developing an alcohol problem or another form of addiction or mental health problems, because of genetics and/or environmental factors.
- Talk to someone in the extended family that you trust.
- Get rid of bitterness and resentment. It is true that such emotions continue to harm and are hard to let go.
- If the children are old enough, consider Alateen for them.
- Ask for some counselling for them from a child psychologist or school counsellor.
- Attend family therapy, if advised to do so.
- Read some literature on alcohol and children and family matters.

The children should be given help in an age-appropriate way.

Frequently asked questions

Will the fact that I am alcoholic go against me in my court battle to gain access and custody of my children?

This is a very difficult question and sadly there is no simple answer. The court will, of course, take your drinking history into consideration but will also take into account your partner's history, bearing in mind the children's long-term safety and well-being, and will err on the side of caution when awarding access or custody. The key factors are whether or not you have now recovered, are not drinking and therefore pose no threat to the children's future health and safety. By definition, if such matters are unable to be negotiated amicably and get as far as court, the process is more likely to be acrimonious and complicated. Allegations may be made on both sides to convince the court that the other party is not a fit parent. Although such issues are rightly raised in many cases, one wonders in other cases how such bitter remarks and beliefs can be helpful to the safety and well-being of the children. Most courts take into account the wishes of the children and often establish what these are by involving a third-party independent childcare expert.

I am sceptical about psychological help as I went to see a therapist some years ago about my wife's drinking and he was very inappropriate in that he spoke about himself most of the time. He told me about his own problems with alcohol in the past in tabloid detail.

I have been asked this question a number of times.

You were unfortunately one of the unlucky ones who happened to meet a therapist who behaved unethically. This is most unusual and you should consider making a complaint, as other people will be exposed to the same person's methods. A therapist should not talk about his or her own personal details, should not impose his or her own history on you, and certainly should not give alarming details. You are there for help, and this is a type of abuse. As regards being sceptical about psychological help, I don't blame you, but I would urge you to try again with someone else. Research it carefully and check out a potential therapist in some detail. Look for a recommendation from someone you trust, such as a GP. Psychological help is vital, in my opinion, for most people, to help them dig themselves out of a rut.

9

What can I do? Practical realities

This chapter is about practical advice for family members caught in the headlights of addiction. There is often nowhere to run because the legs simply don't work as a result of fear or lack of confidence. The person has been crushed emotionally into submission and compliance, and may not even recognize that alcohol is the significant problem.

It is probably a little artificial to talk about practical advice on its own or to distinguish it from emotional help. Therefore this chapter should be read in conjunction with the previous one on psychological and emotional aspects.

So the old question goes, how do you eat an elephant? The answer, of course, is one bite at a time! You have to start somewhere. It may not be easy to change a relationship, but remember that small changes really can make a big difference in the long run.

As an alcohol problem develops, and as the years pass by, partners and family members have to contend with all sorts of other issues that are unrelated to alcohol. Everyday life goes on. People get ill, have to go to school and work, meet the neighbours, suffer bereavements, make new friends and do everyday tasks like going to the shops. Just because you are involved in a relationship with someone who is alcohol-dependent does not make you immune to or detached from the rest of life's joys and upsets.

Of course, alcohol problems do make routines harder to manage and there tends to be much less joy in events that other people perhaps take for granted. Many of the 'sacred' day-to-day activities and one-off family events are ruined because of the presence of a drinking problem.

I use the word 'sacred' because 'ordinary' families enjoy sacred times together – special moments when they enjoy each other's company in a secure environment where each person is equally cherished and respected. At these times, bonding is developed and sentimental family folklore and stories exchanged. Family members are comfortable with each other at these times. They sit down to meals together, are told in all sorts of ways that they are loved, young children are tucked in at night-time and deep conversations occur where advice and support is dispensed. In short, these sacred times are regular, taken-for-granted events in most homes. There is no threat and the family members feel safe. Most people can readily remember events from their childhood that give them a warm glow.

Families should also be able to enjoy birthdays, festive days, graduations, weddings, sporting occasions and other get-togethers. Funerals too are a sacred time where the family gains support and comfort from the local community and the extended family and friends.

Problem drinking often destroys these events. Contrast that sense of well-being, respect and support with the lives of those caught up in alcohol problems. Think perhaps of some of the accounts from children related in Chapter 5. The word 'sacred' can transpose into 'scared' so easily.

One woman who was coping with all sorts of horrific events due to her husband's drinking told me that what she most minded in living with her alcoholic husband was his absence at night-time. She felt this badly for their young children, and in particular the dearth of bedtime stories. This was something she had cherished herself as a young child, and thanks to his erratic appearances at home, the children were never tucked in properly, as she saw it. We are inclined to focus on the more horrific aspects of alcoholism, whereas probably the most damage is done to families by the absence of the 'taken for granted' sacred events that occur in most homes.

Practical self-care

People often confuse self-care with selfishness. Perhaps that is because you have learned to neglect yourself. You may also have been told so many times that you are selfish. But recovery is about taking care of yourself. It is not a one-off event, but an ongoing process that should include listening carefully to your own thoughts and beliefs. It is also about paying attention to and trusting your own instincts. If you manage to take some practical steps you will certainly start to feel better emotionally. The essential component of cognitive behavioural therapy, a popular aspect of counselling, is how your negative thoughts infect your mood and allow you to feel bad about yourself.

There are all sorts of practical steps you can take to improve your circumstances. Some of these are partly repeated from emotional aspects of self-care in the previous chapter but, believe me, they are practical, too:

- Go to an Al-Anon meeting or some equivalent self-help group.
- Ask for legal advice. You do not have to act on it, and free legal advice is available for those who cannot afford private fees.
- Take a break and go away for a while. Remove yourself even temporarily from the stress and strain of living with alcohol problems.
- Talk to a friend or trusted family member.
- Visit a treatment centre and ask them what, if anything, they might be able to do for you.
- Seek out monetary and budgeting advice.
- Use the school guidance and counselling services for help with the children.
- Make a list of things you *need* to do every day and things you *might* do every day.
- Be even a little more assertive, say what you want, with consideration to your personal safety.
- Get a physical check-up. Talk to your GP.
- Do some physical exercise. It will help you to feel better and may also release some pent-up emotions, especially anger.
- Journal your thoughts and feelings. Write down what you are thinking and feeling every day. It might also prove useful if you require evidence of problems at a later date, for a court hearing, for example. Store such writings carefully.
- Read a book on alcohol and some of the many leaflets that are available.
- Enrol on a course.
- Be a tourist in your own area.
- Ring a helpline (see Useful addresses).
- Explore your own past.
- Write your autobiography, with the help of a counsellor.
- Try not to panic. Remember, it is unlikely that things will change dramatically or quickly.
- Again! Do not get entangled in useless arguments with your problem drinker.

It is also important for everyone to realize that nothing stays the same over a period of time.

You do have choices, even if some of them seem unattractive. From a practical point of view, if you are in a relationship with someone in active alcoholism you may have limited options. However, with help you can see that there are indeed choices.

In blunt and practical terms you have five main choices:

1 You can do nothing about trying to improve things for yourself.
2 You can continue the way you have been going, responding or reacting to the latest issue or event as best you can but with no mid- or long-term goals, except that you hope and pray that your partner will somehow miraculously recover and address his drinking. In this situation you are very much a passive victim of your partner's mood, behaviour and future intentions. He is in good form, therefore you are in good form; he is down, therefore you are down, and so on.
3 You can physically separate. This means taking yourself out of the firing line by going to stay with someone for a short time, or by removing yourself from the bedroom, or by not being present when he comes home. Basically this means that you are living in the same home but as though you are separated.
4 You can legally separate or divorce. This is usually a long process that can have many fraught moments en route. Sometimes, though, it is not as difficult as you might think, and in many cases agreement can be reached without too much expense or disruption to everyone's lives.
5 You can decide that you will no longer try to stop him drinking or try to control his behaviour and that all your efforts will now be directed at improving your own coping skills. You will try to heal from the wounds and make a plan over time to improve your situation.

Quite often in counselling, people come with the hope, belief and expectation that the therapist can make their partner stop drinking or give them the skills, tricks and resources to make their partner abstain from alcohol. This is usually not possible, something that has to be carefully and sensitively explained. I usually say to people that they have tried every which way to stop their partner drinking and if they cannot achieve that goal, how could anyone else possibly be successful? Instead, the choices as outlined above are sometimes presented to the person.

This leads to a different type of discussion. Each choice needs to be carefully explored and discussed. Sometimes if you are utterly stuck, as in the first option above, it is hard for you to see that scenario clearly. Naming this choice is so stark that it sometimes helps you to challenge this approach, and perhaps to realize the futility of doing nothing. I tend to say that you cannot change anyone else, but you can possibly create a situation where the other person is capable of change.

Issues after the relationship has ended

Even if you decide to separate, many other issues still need to be addressed. Long after the relationship has 'officially' ended there can be emotional and practical complications. A major problem is finances. Money can be used as leverage to increase or restrict access to children. Stalling tactics are sometimes used too, on both sides of the divide, that only serve to increase legal costs and distress for all concerned.

Many couples get back together for short or long periods of time. They try again, as if they were dating all over again. This may be because of the 'righting or fixing reflex' or because of familiarity or because of love. In many cases, that re-start of the relationship is a disaster because the person with the alcohol problem has not changed his drinking ways, and the fault lines inevitably reappear. Sometimes the drinking problem is sorted and there is an attempt at reconciliation. In these circumstances the relationship can sometimes work. However, the dynamic of the 'previous' relationship will have changed dramatically and adjustments may be difficult to make. The extended family may have difficulty coming to terms with your separation and have their own views about how things should have been handled (or not handled), and how they should proceed.

In most cases, the animosity that caused the separation heals over time and practical realities focus the mind. Most people care deeply about how the children react to the upheaval and try to be reasonable. Rifts can and do appear, however. When the issues are unresolved, the children can be used as pawns and may get very hurt trying to please both parents. Practical realities still abound in regard to the children. If your old partner is still drinking, for example, are the children safe with him?

This adds to the pressure in social situations. If the children are being confirmed or getting married or there is a family funeral, there is a need for some type of choreography around the social norms of such occasions. A lady whose alcoholic partner died many years after they had split told me that when attending his funeral she was *persona non grata*. They both had new partners and she did not feel welcome. Her summary to me about these events was that there are no rules for separated people on such occasions.

Aftermath

If the relationship breaks down despite everyone's best efforts, there are still difficult situations and issues to negotiate in the days, months and years following the separation, whether it be a legal separation or not. The sheer trauma of coming to that big decision is likely to have a huge impact on all concerned. Emptiness and an absence of adrenalin are difficult to live with initially. Loneliness and trauma are common. There is often a sense of failure and maybe guilt and shame because the relationship has finally come to an end. There may be relief too, but this may take some time to make itself felt. There is often considerable anger and bitterness, and sadly this is often expressed in front of the children, who may be put in a position where they have to take sides. The practical custody and access arrangements are often unreliable and awkward at the start but usually evolve into a reasonable, practical arrangement over time.

When your partner dies

People with unresolved alcohol problems tragically often meet with untimely deaths. When death takes place, the partner is often left with painful issues and emotions that need to be carefully and tactfully explored. There is, of course, a sense of loss and grief in every bereavement. Each individual loss is different, though, and there are very personal, unique and specific aspects to resolve. When did you last see or talk to the person? What were the last words you said to each other? Were they angry words? Can you look back on happy times together? Do you have many regrets?

Sadly, usually there are many regrets, cross words have been spoken and there have been periods of excruciating silence. Initially, the bereaved partner may only be able to recall or focus on negative events and incidents. There may be guilt too if the partner has been made to leave the house, or if separation or divorce has taken place.

When the partner with the alcohol problem has taken his own life, these feelings and thoughts are intensified. Other members of your own family or of his family might be very critical of your methods of coping, or indeed of decisions you have taken. If you and your partner had become involved in another relationship, this will have added to the complicated mix of emotions. There may also be relief that your partner has departed, but these feelings are difficult to reconcile.

A lady in her fifties who is now involved in another relationship summed up such emotions thus:

> I know it sounds awful, but before he died I wished he would die so many times. When it eventually came to pass I was honestly so relieved and it felt like the burden had been lifted off me. I did not cry at the

funeral and I did not even want to be there. People were coming up to me sympathizing and saying stupid things like what a great guy he was. I was thinking, 'If only you knew.' I know that it was a legitimate feeling to want him to die when he was alive. I was treated so badly by him but I feel so guilty about it now, six months on, and wonder if I could have done anything else to help him. We had good times way back.

Frequently asked questions

My husband has started to drink again after many years of abstinence when there was great healing and all was forgiven. Now I am devastated and all the old hurts and incidents are re-emerging. I kicked him out of the house. I would like to have him back but I am very afraid of the future and not sure if I want to continue the relationship.

Relapses are always a real possibility in the lives of alcoholics and their partners. Generally speaking, the longer the period of abstinence, the better the outcome; however, there is always a danger of returning to a destructive pattern of drinking. When someone relapses after a long period of sobriety it raises all the old hurts and almost inevitably leads to soul-searching for all concerned. The most important issue here is to get help for yourself so that you can process the mixed-up emotions that you are going through. Your partner should also be encouraged to get help. He may be reluctant for all sorts of reasons, including damaged pride, guilt and shame. Consult an experienced therapist. In most cases after long-term sobriety the person can recover and go back to abstinence after getting some form of help or treatment, though sadly in some cases this isn't possible. The bigger issue of whether or not you should stay in the relationship needs to be addressed later. You need to do some work on yourself and also have a bit of space before these difficult decisions are tackled.

My husband is an alcoholic. He was recently treated in a residential facility and so far is doing really well. Should I keep alcohol at home? Is it too much of a temptation for him?

Understandably, people in these circumstances are consumed by such practical realities and some of these have been discussed in this chapter. The question can only be resolved by discussion and an attempt to work out what is best in individual instances. Different couples handle this in various ways. In most cases in the early days of recovery people are usually advised to avoid drinking situations and occasions if at all possible until they find their feet. For people like publicans, this is of course impossible if they continue to work in this area. There is no reason to believe that success rates for publicans are any different from other occupations, so it would seem logical to assume that access to alcohol is not a key factor in most cases of relapse.

In today's society it is almost impossible to avoid all drinking occasions for ever. Alcohol is part of most happy and sad events. People in recovery have to learn how to handle such occasions and to protect their own recovery. It would be naive to think that not keeping alcohol at home would solve the problem or stop the person from drinking long term, as there are so many retail outlets and alcohol is widely available. People often ask, too, 'Should I drink with the person in recovery?' Once again, this should involve discussion but most people in recovery are quite happy for their partner to drink in their company provided, of course, she does not have an active alcohol problem herself. People in recovery are often uncomfortable if their loved ones do not drink in front of them, especially if this was the practice before they themselves stopped drinking.

10

Conclusions

This book has attempted to describe the impact of problem drinking on families, but with particular reference to the partner. Countless numbers of people are living – or, more likely, barely surviving – with active alcoholism. They are coping with inconsistency at best and terror at worst. They are therefore living in the proximity of alcoholic volcanoes and regularly getting badly burned from frequent eruptions without any perceived prospect or hope of being rescued. They do their best to try to contain the fall-out for all concerned within the family circle. Their lives involve being badly hurt, dusting themselves off and being badly hurt all over again. There is no sense of security and the only sense of predictability for many people is that it will happen again. At any point, their lives are thrown into confusion and mayhem. I sincerely hope that this book will provide more hope that good help is available and that there are things that can be done to improve your current situation.

The book has also attempted to explain another side of this complex story. The question has been asked: do family relationships sometimes contribute to the development or continuation of an alcohol problem? Is it the case that some people are in such unhappy relationships that their only sense of protest or autonomy is to drink to excess? Alcohol dependence and any other form of addiction have the paradoxical property of being able to square circles in the short term. Some people consciously or unconsciously get so embroiled in attempts to control their partner and their partner's drinking that, at the very least, they add to the problem. Others contribute to alcohol problems through their behaviour or by dark ulterior motives. In some weird or twisted way their needs are met by some dynamic within the relationship that makes them feel superior or in control. The '****U syndrome' has also been explored (Chapter 6), where deep anger and resentment fuels someone's drinking in a very unhappy relationship.

Perhaps in all cases there is a little bit of 'secondary gain' involved, where some form of pay-out occurs even though there is also a price to pay, and those who are successful in sorting out their problems gain insight into these areas. These matters need to be very sensitively handled if partners are not to be further traumatized during therapy.

In any event and in all cases, help is available and people should be encouraged to seek out that help and find ways of coping or of getting away from the problem. It is so easy to get stuck in a rut and accept behaviour and events that are unacceptable. If you can identify with that sense of being stuck, then this is the time to look for assistance.

Family dynamics and the plight of the partner in alcoholic relationships receive little attention in society and even less in the training of most health professionals. With notable exceptions, healthcare professionals receive paltry input in these areas during their training, despite the fact that such problems take up a large part of their workload when they are qualified.

Alcohol problems are very common in our society. Our Western world tends to accept the abnormal as normal when it is common. Many people are addicted to some substance or other and their partners suffer the consequences. A significant number of health professionals, during the course of their lives, suffer from alcohol problems too. This can be a barrier to helping patients or, in the case of those who manage a full recovery, an advantage to patients who need help.

Of course, ideally there should be routine screening and counselling for alcohol problems in all healthcare facilities. Certain symptoms among patients and family members should raise concerns and suspicions that there might be an alcohol problem in the family. For example, everyone who presents with sleep disturbances, headaches, anxiety or depression might merit a discussion about lifestyle issues including alcohol use. Ideally, too, all GP patients and their families should have access to high-quality free counselling. Family members and particularly children are neglected by many of the mainstream services, yet if proper training and resources were provided a great deal could be done to help them significantly. Ultimately the provision of such services would save money, and governments should be encouraged to take the longer-term financial savings viewpoint even if they are not persuaded by simple arguments about the improvement of health and well-being.

There are numerous simple and complex dilemmas in relationships as a result of alcohol problems. Each individual strand of such enmeshed problems requires intricate work to disentangle and resolve. Many people face desperately difficult decisions, or feel hopelessly trapped in damaging, abusive relationships. Yet there is a lot of help available and people do get better and extricate themselves from terrible situations. Individual partners and family members recover. Couples recover too.

To paraphrase the great American golfing coach, Bob Rotella, 'Life is not a game of perfect.' All you can do with the hand that you have been dealt is to do your very best with it. If you have an alcohol problem, at least you *know* that you are not perfect. You are human, however, and capable of change. If you are the partner or sibling or parent or friend of someone with an alcohol problem, you too are capable of making changes, and by so doing may create an opportunity for the person with the alcohol problem to make effective changes too. No doubt mistakes will be made on your journey to recovery, so when they happen do not beat yourself up: accept them, try your very best to learn from them and on you go again.

Gerry and Mary are a good positive example to finish with.

They met, as many couples do, in their late teens and got married in their twenties. Gerry developed an alcohol problem that was probably there from shortly after he started drinking, aged 15, and there was hell to pay in their relationship for about six years before he got help. He took his courage in both hands and went into a residential facility. It was hard and they both had to face many painful truths in therapy. They did after-care together for about a year, and also some relationship therapy. So far he is 20 years sober and they have only had to contend with the usual life events, day-to-day issues, worries and minor rows. They have three children and all is well.

Happily, many thousands of couples are in this situation, and the majority of these success stories did not have to go to in-house facilities for treatment, though the vast majority will have received some form of outside help. Obviously this would be my wish for readers, but 'success', as explained, can also mean many other things, including physical, emotional or legal separation.

As the saying goes, 'It is where it is.' You are unable to change the past and your effort must be to accept where it is at the present time and find ways to improve the future. Changing things for the better is rarely impossible.

If you are surviving with alcohol problems and about to put this book down, the final summarized message is that people are very resourceful and *can* live with all sorts of difficulties, but you do not *have to* accept behaviour that is unacceptable and you certainly can access help. That process is not usually quick, but if you stick with it you can 'unstick' yourself from the worst aspects of alcohol problems.

The goal is to live rather than to survive.

Appendix: The Serenity Prayer

The Serenity Prayer has become known as the prayer of Alcoholics Anonymous (AA) but is used by everyone affected by alcohol problems. The first four lines are most often spoken at AA meetings but perhaps should be used by everyone. The 'living one day at a time' philosophy is also most important and a good life template for everyone to aspire to. 'God' does not have to be a religious God in this context but whatever higher power you might believe in – for example, nature.

> God grant me the serenity
> to accept the things I cannot change;
> courage to change the things I can;
> and wisdom to know the difference.
> Living one day at a time;
> enjoying one moment at a time;
> accepting hardships as the pathway to peace;
> taking, as He did, this sinful world
> as it is, not as I would have it;
> trusting that He will make all things right
> if I surrender to His Will;
> that I may be reasonably happy in this life
> and supremely happy with Him
> forever in the next.
> Amen.
>
> (Reinhold Niebuhr)

Useful addresses

Please note the following is only a selection of numerous agencies that are of help to people in the United Kingdom and Ireland. Most of the ones listed are free. For advice on specific counselling services ask a professional in healthcare, such as your GP.

UK

Alcohol Concern
64 Leman Street
London E1 8EU
Tel.: 020 7264 0510
Website: www.alcoholconcern.org.uk
This organization provides extensive services, including information on treatment in your locality, and numerous leaflets.

Alcoholics Anonymous
General Service Office
PO Box 1, Toft Green
York YO1 7NJ
National Helpline: 0845 769 7555
Website: www.alcoholicsanonymous.org.uk
Meetings are held in every local area in the UK and Ireland (see page 105). All you need is an honest desire to stop drinking, then just turn up. If you know someone in the fellowship he/she might be willing to take you along. AA has a sponsor system and also helps participants to work through AA's particular 12-step programme.

Al-Anon and Alateen Family Groups (UK and Eire)
61 Great Dover Street
London SE1 4YF
Tel.: 020 7403 0888 (confidential helpline); 020 7407 0215 (Alateen)
Websites: www al-anonuk.org.uk; www.al-anonuk.org.uk/alateen
Al-Anon provides support groups throughout the UK and Ireland for adult family members of people living with alcoholism. Alateen is for the teenage children of alcoholics.

Barnardos UK
National Office
Tanners Lane, Barkingside
Ilford, Essex IG6 1QG
Tel.: 020 8550 8822
Website: www.barnardos.org.uk

ChildLine UK
National Helpline: 0800 11 11
Website: www.childline.org.uk

Citizens Advice (operating name of the **National Association of Citizens Advice Bureaux**)
Website: www.citizensadvice.org.uk
A great source of information when searching for self-help groups, support agencies and organizations in the UK and Ireland (where they are known as **Citizens Information**: see page 106). They can also provide advice on money and budgeting. For a phone number, consult a local phone directory or Yellow Pages.

Community Legal Advice
Tel.: 0845 345 4345
Website: www.communitylegaladvice.org.uk
Gives advice and help on free legal advice and aid.

Cruse Bereavement UK
Tel.: 0844 477 9400 (daytime helpline); 020 8939 9530 (administration)
Website: www.crusebereavementcare.org.uk
Offers help for those experiencing bereavement.

Depression Alliance
20 Great Dover Street
London SE1 4LX
Tel.: 0845 123 23 20 (for information pack only; not a helpline)
Website: www.depressionalliance.org

ManKind
Tel.: 01823 334244 (national helpline 10 a.m. to 4 p.m./ 7 p.m. to 9 p.m., Mondays to Fridays)
Website: www.mankind.org.uk
Provides assistance for men who experience domestic violence.

National Association of Children of Alcoholics (NACOA)
PO Box 64
Fishponds
Bristol BS16 2UH
National Helpline: 0800 358 3456
Website: www.nacoa.org.uk

National Family Mediation
Margaret Jackson Centre
4 Barnfield Hill
Exeter EX1 1SR
Tel.: 01392 271610
Website: www.nfm.org.uk
Mediation services help people to separate without huge costs, and also do what they can to ensure that children are able to keep in contact with one or both parents.

Rape Crisis Centres
Website: www.rapecrisis.org.uk
The site lists centres and phone numbers in England and Wales. They also give advice on all aspects of sexual assault. For Scotland, there is a national helpline (08088 01 03 02, 6 p.m. to midnight; www. rapecrisisscotland.org.uk). In Northern Ireland there is a centre in Belfast (Tel.: 028 9032 9002; www.rapecrisisni.com).

Samaritans (UK and Ireland)
Chris
PO Box 9090
Stirling FK8 2SA
Tel.: 08457 90 90 90 (UK); 1850 60 90 90 (Irish Republic)
Website: www.samaritans.org

Survivors of Bereavement by Suicide (formerly SOBS)
Flamsteed Centre
Albert Street
Ilkeston
Derbyshire DE7 5GU
National Helpline: 0844 561 6855 (9 a.m. to 9 p.m.); 0115 944 1117
Website: www.uk-sobs.org.uk

Treatment agencies for alcohol
These are far too numerous (in Ireland and the UK) to list but advice can be received from your local general practice or primary care centre, from national helplines on alcohol, from the National Health Service in the UK and the Health Service Executive in Ireland.

Women's Aid UK
Helpline: 0808 2000 247
Website: www.womensaid.org.uk
A national charity working to end domestic violence against women and children. In Northern Ireland it is known as the Women's Aid Federation (website: www.niwaf.org).

Irish Republic

Alcoholics Anonymous
General Service Office
Unit 2, Block C
Santry Business Park
Swords Road
Dublin 9
Tel.: (00) 353 1 842 0700
Website: www.alcoholics-anonymous.ie

Al-Anon and Alateen Ireland
Information Centre
Room 5, 5 Caple Street
Dublin 1
Tel.: (00) 353 1 873 2699 (10.30 a.m. to 2.30 p.m., Monday to Friday)
Website: www.al-anon-ireland.org

Alcohol Action Ireland
Butler Court
25 Great Strand Street
Rear, Dublin 1
Tel.: (00) 353 1 878 0610
Website: www.alcoholireland.ie
This group is very similar in many ways to Alcohol Concern UK. They
have published an information leaflet, *Is drinking affecting your family?*
(2009).

Amen, Ireland
Tel.: 046 9023718 (out of hours 086 7941 880)
Website: www.amen.ie
Provides a confidential helpline and support service for male victims of
domestic abuse and their children.

Aware
National Office
72 Lower Leeson Street
Dublin 2
Tel.: 01 661 7211 (general enquiries); 1890 303 302 (national helpline).
Website: www.aware.ie
A national voluntary organization for those with depression, providing,
among other services, support groups.

Barnardos
National Office
Christchurch Square
Dublin 8
Tel.: 01 453 0355
Website: www.barnardos.ie

Bereavement Counselling Service
Admin Office
Dublin Street
Baldoyle, Dublin 13
Tel.: 1839 1766 (9 a.m. to 1 p.m., Monday to Friday)
Website: www.bereavementireland.com
There are additional offices in Dublin (see website), but this admin office
provides a booklet, *Grieving the Suicide of a Loved One*.

Childline Ireland
National Helpline: 1800 66 66 66
Website: www.childline.ie

Citizens Information
Similar to Citizens Advice in the UK; run by the Citizens Information
Board. They will provide advice on money and budgeting, among other
services.
Tel.: 1890 777 121
Website: www.citizensinformation.ie

Console, Ireland
National Helpline: 1800 201 890
This organization assists those who have been bereaved as a result of
a suicide. It has also helped to establish 1Life, a free national 24-hour
helpline for those who are in suicidal distress: 1800 247 100.

Dublin Rape Crisis Centre
National Helpline: 1800 788 888
Website: www.drcc.ie

Family Mediation Service
First Floor, St Stephen's Green House
Earlsfort Terrace
Dublin 2
Tel.: 01 634 4320
They will provide details of other full-time offices dealing with family
mediation in Cork, Galway and Limerick, and part-time ones in other
towns and cities across Ireland. There are also private mediators who can
be attended.

Family Support Agency
Fourth Floor, St Stephen's Green House
Earlsfort Terrace
Dublin 2
Tel.: 01 611 4100
Website: www.fsa.ie
Provides help and advice on a range of topics, including Irish mediation
services (see also **Family Mediation Service** immediately above, with
whom they share the website).

Free Legal Advice Centres, Ireland
13 Lower Dorset Street
Dublin 1
Tel.: 1890 350 250 (information and referral)
Website: www.flac.ie

Money Advice and Budgeting Service (MABS)
Administrator, MABS National Development Ltd
Second Floor, Commercial House
Westend Commercial Village
Blanchardstown
Dublin 15
Tel.: 01 812 9500 (information)
National Helpline: 1890 283 438
Website: www.mabs.ie
For help and advice; see also **Citizens Information** (page 106).

Women's Aid, Ireland
Tel.: 01 868 4721 (general enquiries)
National Helpline for those at risk: 1800 341 900
Website: www.womensaid.ie

References and further reading

Anderson, P. et al., *Clinical Guidelines on Identification and Brief Interventions*. Department of Health of the Government of Catalonia, Barcelona, 2005. (Note: these clinical guidelines were developed as part of the Primary Health Care European Projects on Alcohol (PHEPA) funded by the EU, and they contain much information on brief interventions. Visit <www.phepa.net> for more information.)

Anderson, R. et al., *Alcohol Aware Practice Service Initiative*, final report. Irish College of General Practitioners, Dublin, 2006.

Beattie, M., *Codependent No More*. Hazelden, Center City, MN, 1992.

Bermingham, J., *A Memoir of the Very Reverend Theobald Mathew*. Milliken and Sons, Dublin, 1840.

Capello, A. et al., 'Methods for reducing alcohol and drug-related family harm in non-specialist settings', *Journal of Mental Health* (2000), 9 (3): 329–43.

Cooney, J. G., *Under the Weather*, second edition. Newleaf, Dublin, 2002.

Institute of Medicine, *Broadening the Base of Treatment*. National Academic Press, Washington DC, 1990.

Murphy, Y., *Report by the Commission of Investigation into the Catholic Archdiocese of Dublin* (The Murphy Report). Government Publications, Dublin, 2009.

Peterson, C., Maher, S. and Seligman, M., *Learned Helplessness: A Theory for the Age of Personal Control*. Oxford University Press, New York, 1993.

Prochaska, J. and DiClemente, C., 'Transtheorethical therapy: towards a more integrative model of change', *Psychotherapy Theory and Practice* (1982), 19: 276–88.

Rotella, B., *Golf is Not a Game of Perfect*. Simon and Schuster, New York, 1995.

Ryan, S., *Commission to Enquire into Child Abuse* (The Ryan Report). Government Publications, Dublin, 2009.

Scott, Walter, *Marmion*. J. Ballantyne, Edinburgh, 1808.

Strategy Unit, *Alcohol Harm Reduction Strategy for England*. Government Publications, London, 2004.

Wegscheider Cruse, S., *Family Reconstruction: The Living Theatre Model*. Science and Behavior Books, Palo Alto, CA, 1997.

Whalen, T., 'Wives of alcoholics: four types observed in a family agency', *Quarterly Journal of Studies on Alcohol* (1953), 14: 1632–41.

Index

Prochaska, James 82–3
professional help 70–1
see counselling; therapy

recovery
family/couple therapy 86–7
forgiveness and 19–20
lapses and relapses 83, 95
simple steps towards 84–6
wheel of change 78–9
resentment
of children 87
after stopping 46–7
responsibility
disease model and 3, 4
Rotella, Bob 99

Scott, Sir Walter 66
self-esteem 65, 84–5
abuse by criticism 11
feeling like zero 20
sex and 32
self-harm 11
self-help groups 74–6, 84
Serenity Prayer 84, 101
sexual matters
abuse of children 55–6
alcohol-caused issues 32
children and 57
drinking as solution for 63
escaping from problems 68
partner's problems 17
violence and 71
violent demands 30

sexually transmitted illnesses (STIs)
8, 32
sleep disturbance 15
social relations
avoiding events 27
joining in for drinking 61–2
partner's fear and 12
Stockholm syndrome 45
suicide
fear of 31
partners 11
threatening 23

therapy 85–6
unethical therapists 88
see also counselling
tough love 43–4, 46
treatment centres 76–8, 91
trust breakdown 17

violence 31
abstaining and 7
challenging and 41
coexisting problems 33–4
as a sign 27
varieties of 18

Wegscheider, Sharon 59
wheel of change 78–9
wishful thinking 18–19
withdrawal
defining dependence 6–7
work 27
worrying 15